G000114295

German Annual of Spatial Research and Policy

Editors:

ARL – Academy for Spatial Research and Planning, Hanover
BBSR – Federal Institute for Research on Building, Urban Affairs and Spatial
Development, Bonn
IfL – Leibniz Institute for Regional Geography, Leipzig
IOER – Leibniz Institute of Ecological and Regional Development, Dresden
IRS – Leibniz Institute for Regional Development and Structural Planning, Erkner

Responsible for the 2010 edition:

IOER – Leibniz Institute of Ecological and Regional Development, Dresden

Recently published in this series:

Sebastian Lentz, Editor:
German Annual of Spatial Research and Policy 2006
Restructuring Eastern Germany
ISBN 978-3-540-32077-7

Dietmar Scholich, Editor:
German Annual of Spatial Research and Policy 2007
Territorial Cohesion
ISBN 978-3-540-71745-4

Wendelin Strubelt, Editor:
German Annual of Spatial Research and Policy 2008
Guiding Principles for Spatial Development in Germany
ISBN 978-3-540-88838-3

Heiderose Kilper, Editor:
German Annual of Spatial Research and Policy 2009
New Disparities in Spatial Development in Europe
ISBN 978-3-642-03401-5

Bernhard Müller, Editor:
German Annual of Spatial Research and Policy 2010
Urban Regional Resilience: How Do Cities and Regions Deal with Change?
ISBN 978-3-642-12784-7

Bernhard Müller (Ed.)

Urban Regional Resilience: How Do Cities and Regions Deal with Change?

With 19 Figures

 Springer

Editor
Prof. Dr. Dr. h. c. Bernhard Müller
Leibniz Institute of Ecological
and Regional Development (IOER)
Weberplatz 1
01217 Dresden
Germany
www.ioer.de

The German Annual contains scientific articles that have been reviewed according to international standards, as well as short reports about research and practical experience.

Editorial staff:
ts|pk, Berlin: Christoph Rosenkranz

English language editors:
David Skogley, Kleinmachnow
Sandra Lustig, Hamburg

Layout:
Karin Engelke, Berlin

Picture credits, front cover:
Lower image: ©ESPON, 2013; Aggregated Hazard Map
Upper image: ©IOER, B. Heber, 2001; Aerial Photo Dresden

Picture credits, back cover:
© IOER, 2001; Collaborative Planning

ISSN 1862-5738   e-ISSN 1862-572X
ISBN 978-3-642-12784-7   e-ISBN 978-3-642-12785-4
DOI 10.1007/978-3-642-12785-4
Springer Heidelberg Dordrecht London New York

© Springer-Verlag Berlin Heidelberg 2011
This work is subject to copyright. All rights are reserved, whether the whole or part of the material is concerned, specifically the rights of translation, reprinting, reuse of illustrations, recitation, broadcasting, reproduction on microfilm or in any other way, and storage in data banks. Duplication of this publication or parts thereof is permitted only under the provisions of the German Copyright Law of September 9, 1965, in its current version, and permission for use must always be obtained from Springer. Violations are liable to prosecution under the German Copyright Law.
The use of general descriptive names, registered names, trademarks, etc. in this publication does not imply, even in the absence of a specific statement, that such names are exempt from the relevant protective laws and regulations and therefore free for general use.

Cover design: eStudio Calamar S.L.

Printed on acid-free paper

Springer is part of Springer Science+Business Media (www.springer.com)

Acknowledgement

With the German Annual of Spatial Research and Policy 2010, a joint five year project comes to an end. The five participating institutions, the Academy for Spatial Research and Planning (ARL), the Federal Institute for Research on Building, Urban Affairs and Spatial Development (BBSR), the Leibniz Institute for Regional Geography (IfL), as well as the Leibniz Institute for Regional Development and Structural Planning (IRS), and the Leibniz Institute of Ecological and Regional Development (IOER), have worked together since 2006 to provide an international audience with some insight into spatial research and policy in Germany. In the future special English-language issues of the journal 'Raumforschung und Raumordnung' will take over this function. I would like to express my gratitude to all those who helped to make this fascinating project possible.

Regarding the German Annual 2010, I would like to thank all the authors who have contributed to his publication: Sonja Deppisch, Mareike Schaerffer, Stephan Schmidt, Enke Franck, and Sebastian Ebert from the ARL; Fabian Dosch, Lars Porsche, Manfred Fuhrich, and Evi Goderbauer from the BBSR; Joachim Burdack, Bastian Lange, and Thilo Lang from the IfL; Ludger Gailing, Andreas Röhring, Heiderose Kilper, Torsten Thurmann, Andreas Vetter, Frank Sondershaus, Susen Fischer, and Manfred Kühn from the IRS; Gérard Hutter, Thomas Naumann, Reinhard Schinke, Johannes Nikolowski, Sebastian Golz, Alfred Olfert, Jana Planek, Andreas Blum, and Karin Gruhler from the IOER.

For evaluating the articles in this publication I would like to thank my colleagues and distinguished experts: Arthur Benz (FernUniversität Hagen, Germany), Marco Bontje (University of Amsterdam, Netherlands), Franz Brunner (University of Graz, Austria), Thomas Elmqvist (Stockholm University, Sweden), Dietrich Fürst (University of Hanover, Germany), Matthias Koziol (BTU Cottbus, Germany), Thomas Kuder (vhw - Bundesverband für Wohnen und Stadtentwicklung e.V., Berlin, Germany), Vinzent Nadin (Delft University of Technology, Netherlands), Stefan Reese (National Institute of Water and Atmospheric Research Ltd., Wellington, New Zealand), Claus-C. Wiegandt (University of Bonn, Germany), and Markus Wissen (University of Vienna, Austria).

For co-editing this publication I would also like to thank Heiderose Kilper, Hans H. Blotevogel, Elke Pahl-Weber, and Sebastian Lentz. Further thanks go to Christoph Rosenkranz from ts|pk in Berlin. Finally I would like to thank Hendrikje Wehnert for her energetic and very efficient coordination of this publication.

Bernhard Müller

Contents

Thomas Naumann, Johannes Nikolowski, Sebastian Golz, Reinhard Schinke
**Resilience and Resistance of Buildings and Built Structures
to Flood Impacts – Approaches to Analysis and Evaluation   89**

Gérard Hutter
**Planning for Risk Reduction and Organizing for Resilience
in the Context of Natural Hazards   101**

Short Reports

Urban and Regional Resilience – A New Catchword or a Consistent Concept for Research and Practice?

Remarks Concerning the International Debate and the German Discussion

Bernhard Müller[1]

Resilience – Understanding Better How to Deal with Change?

Resilience seems to have become the new catchword of our times. "Resilience is to the 2000s and 2010s what sustainability was to the 1980s and 1990s" (Foster, n.d.). The term is highly attractive as, in general, to be resilient refers to something positive: to be able to withstand hardship and disturbance, to recover from disaster and destruction, to regain one's original shape after deformation, to be cautious enough to prepare for the unforeseen, and to deal with risks in an appropriate way. A high degree of resilience is related to a low degree of vulnerability. The attention the term receives may be "a response to a generalized contemporary sense of uncertainty and insecurity and a search for formulas for adaptation and survival" (Christopherson, Michie, & Tyler, 2010).

This is definitely true for the international debate. However, it is neither an accurate nor complete description of the ongoing discussion in Germany. The German translation of the term, 'Resilienz', is not a common word in colloquial language. Until recently, experts mainly used it in psychology, and resilience research (Resilienzforschung) was almost exclusively seen as a subject of psychology and social pedagogy. This has only changed slowly as the word enters other spheres of discussion. Among them are ecology and environmental sciences as well as – and foremost – risk management and disaster prevention, for example, with regard to floods, storms, and other natural hazards. The intensive debate about climate change in Germany as well as related mitigation and adaptation strategies have recently had a strong influence on the popularization of the term.

Birkmann (2008), for example, as well as Greiving and Fleischauer (2009) conceptualize resilience in association with the discussion about climate change and disaster management. Birkmann looks at the vulnerability of society and that of different land uses. Greiving and Fleischauer (2009, p. 18) even see resilience and a "resilient society" as an overall vision and guiding principle for future urban development in Germany that is related to the necessary adaptation to climate change. Similarly, the *German Committee for Disaster Reduction* (DKKV), the national platform and competence center for disaster risk reduction, promotes the

---

1 Special thanks to Paulina Schiappacasse from TU Dresden and Universidad de Chile, who has considerably inspired and enriched this article through her ongoing research in urban and regional resilience.

B. Müller, *German Annual of Spatial Research and Policy 2010*,
German Annual of Spatial Research and Policy,
DOI 10.1007/978-3-642-12785-4_1, © Springer-Verlag Berlin Heidelberg 2011

enhancement of resilience related to natural hazards. It follows an interdisciplinary approach drawing members and experts from different disciplines and spheres of society in its efforts to pool disaster reduction expertise.

The German focus on climate change and the reduction of natural disasters is in line with what happens in the international arena, where resilience has become a prominent topic especially within the debate about climate change. For example, the first global forum on this topic the 'Resilient Cities 2010' congress in Bonn, Germany, was geared towards enabling exchange, learning, networking, and debate and policy development on approaches and solutions to climate change adaptation for cities and local governments (ICLEI, 2010). Well in line with the 'Making Cities Resilient Campaign' of the 'United Nations International Strategy for Disaster Reduction' in 2010/2011, most participants at the conference focused on disaster prevention strategies, and how efforts to reduce disaster risk can contribute to making cities safer.

However, vulnerability and the ability to recover from disturbances are not merely confined to natural hazards and climate change. They are much broader and multi-facetted issues. A visit to Detroit, Cleveland, Pittsburgh, or Youngstown in the United States, to Manchester or Liverpool in England, to the Rhine-Ruhr metropolis or many medium-sized and smaller cities in Germany, or to cities and regions in the transformation countries of Central, Eastern and Southeastern Europe (cf. Müller, Finka, & Lintz, 2005) reveals at least one other facet of the vulnerability of urban areas and the challenge of urban and regional resilience. Wherever cities are drawn into a downward spiral of urban decline – may it be through economic crisis, deindustrialization, the loss of jobs, social and political transformation, outmigration or demographic change – it is hard for them to recover, to operate and provide services under conditions of distress, to retrofit aging buildings and neighborhoods, or to reorganize and eventually reinvent themselves. This calls for a broader understanding of the term resilience.

A new study commissioned by the *Department for Spatial Planning and Regional Policy Coordination* of the *Austrian Chancellery* (Lukesch, Payer, & Winkler-Rieder, 2010) points in the same direction with regard to the state of discussion in the context of regional development and the possibilities of applying resilience concepts to regional policy in Austria. The authors look at three regions and trace their response patterns and strategies for overcoming shocks and disturbances in order to derive general recommendations for further research and experimental actions in Austria. They emphasize the close relationship between regional resilience as a "steering model", the region as a "socio-economic-cultural-political fabric" based on sustainability and equity, and regional governance. They recommend the application of concepts and models of resilience research to regional development policy and regional governance in Austria.

Looking at the results of the Austrian study in more detail, one may detect certain similarities between the Austrian discussion about regional resilience and the German discussion about sustainable development. This is not surprising as there are many links between resilience and sustainability. Some authors even suggest that resilience should be regarded as the key to sustainable development. "To sustain development in a world in transformation, policy must enhance resilience and sustain social-ecological systems in the face of surprise, unpredictability and complexity" (Swedish Environmental Advisory Council, 2009).

A recent issue of the Cambridge Journal of Regions, Economy and Society (Pendall, Foster, & Cowell, 2010, pp. 71-84) entitled "The Resilient Region", paints a similar picture with regards to looking at resilience from a much broader perspective than studies oriented towards natural hazards and climate change. It explores the resilience concept from a variety of angles and demonstrates "why it has emerged as a popular, albeit contested, concept in environmental studies and social sciences" (Christopherson, Michie, & Tyler, 2010, p. 3). As the world becomes less and less predictable (and we need to accept that change is a dominant part of this), the challenge cities and regions face is how to deal with change. The discussion about resilience may help decision-makers, inhabitants, and other stakeholders involved in urban and regional development find appropriate solutions.

Resilience – More than just a Dazzling Term?

Regarding ecological and social-ecological systems, much reference is made to Holling's influential writings. In his article "Resilience and Stability of Ecological Systems" he differentiates between "stability, which represents the ability of a system to return to an equilibrium state after a temporary disturbance", and "resilience, that is a measure of the persistence of systems and of their ability to absorb change and disturbance and still maintain the same relationships between populations or state variables" (Holling, 1973, p. 15).

Since Holling's article in 1973, there has been much discussion about the role of resilience, panarchy, adaptive capacity, and adaptive management in social-ecological systems. For example, Folke (2006) describes resilience as the "self-organization capacity of a (social) system while undergoing (ecosystem) change so as to maintain the same function and structure". Referring to recovery after disasters, Vale and Campanella (2005) understand resilience as the "relationship between recovery of the built environment and other ways to 'return to normalcy'". In an even broader sense, Ultramari and Rezende (2007, p. 51) connect resilience with the "ability to transform and retransform urban spaces".

The enormous complexity of cities and regions defies a simple concept and approach regarding urban and regional resilience. According to Carpenter et al. (2001), a major methodological challenge for resilience research and its practical application is clarity. When dealing with resilience "we must begin by clearly defining resilience in terms of what to what. These aspects change, depending on the temporal, social, and spatial scale" at which we deal with resilience (Carpenter et al., 2001, p. 767).

Referring to the "resilience of what", the Resilience Alliance (2007) distinguishes between four issues of relevance for (which need further scrutiny) in urban areas:

(a) Metabolic flows in sustaining urban functions, human well-being and the quality of life,
(b) Governance networks and the ability of the society to learn, adapt, and re-organize the way they cope with urban challenges,
(c) The social dynamic of people as citizens, consumers, and users, and,
(d) The built environment that defines the urban physical pattern.

Referring to "resilience to what", we may distinguish between a number of (unexpected) shocks, crises, or events which may push a city-region over a recovery threshold, where it becomes extremely difficult to 'bounce' back. The disturbances to which city-regions tend to be subjected may fall into the following categories: natural (e.g., earthquakes, volcanic eruptions, floods), economic (e.g., market shocks, financial crises), biomedical (e.g., diseases), social (e.g., preference changes, population issues, labor availability, security), technological (e.g., industrial accidents), and political (e.g., change of government, terrorism, wars).

Despite the fact that there is a broad scale of potential shocks, and challenges of precautionary risk reduction strategies, preventive measures, and disaster management, we have to agree with Foster (2006) who notes that disturbances do not automatically have to be negative. They may also be positive. For example, a major new investment or a mega-event may force a city or a region to radically reconsider its development strategy.

Disturbances may vary in temporal and spatial scale. They may occur for a few minutes (e.g., traffic jams), hours and days (e.g., floods, hurricanes), weeks (e.g., stock market crashes), months (e.g., market cycles in housing prices), or even decades (e.g., drought, climate change, warming periods, gentrification). We must distinguish between them and "slow burns" which are typical for systems undergoing transformation (Foster, 2006; Pendall, Foster, & Cowell, 2010); for example a heavy industrialized area shifting its economic base to biotechnology in the face of long-term deindustrialization. While shocks may bring people together, "slow burns" may increase competition for shifting resources, creating winners and losers.

Disturbances may also vary in their spatial scale, i.e., from household, neighbor-hood, and local level activities to a citywide, regional, national, and global scale. As Cumming et al. (2006) hypothesized, many of the problems encountered by societies in management arise because of a mismatch between the scale of institutional management and the scale of the (ecological) processes being managed.

Some authors identify resilience as one of the key issues of the future (Levin et al., 1998; Perrings, 2002), if not even as a guideline for a theory of sustainable development (Kates et al., 2001; Foley et al., 2005). In this line of discussion, some scholars' writing about resilience proposes a more comprehensive understanding of the interactions among ecological, social, political, and economic systems at their different levels of scale (Gunderson & Holling, 2001; Berkes et al., 2003), promoting research efforts across disciplines and together with practitioners. However, they are not unanimously applauded as conceptual clarity and practical relevance are considered to be endangered. According to Brand and Jax (2007) the original descriptive and ecological meaning of resilience has been diluted as the term is meanwhile used for a broad range of topics.

Nevertheless, there are many authors and institutions who have started to transfer resilience thinking to urban and regional development. Christopherson, Michie, and Tyler (2010) provide an ample view on this for regions. Lukesch, Payer, and Winkler-Rieder (2010, p. 4) "put up a steering model for regional resilience which they define as the ability of a socio-economic region, to absorb endogenous or exogenous disturbances by change processes, so that the main functions, structures and relationships being essential for the well-being and the sustainability of the region remain intact."

Newman, Beatley, and Boyer (2009) apply resilience concepts to cities. Cities "need to last, to respond to crises, and adapt in a way that may cause them to change and grow differently; cities require an inner strength, a resolve, as well as a strong physical infrastructure and built environment" (Newman, Beatley, & Boyer, 2009, p. 1). Some institutions, such as the *Center for Resilient Cities* in the United States have chosen resilience as an umbrella term for planning and design strategies needed in order to help cities develop capacities to meet future challenges.

There are at least three weaknesses of the attempts to extend the resilience concept to cities and regions. One is related to their theoretical foundation. The widely spread definition of Alberti et al. (2003), according to which urban resilience is "the degree to which a city is able to tolerate alteration before reorganizing around a new set of structures and processes" may be seen as a good starting point but it is still too broad for a concise and well-founded theoretical concept. Therefore, it is necessary and expedient, to develop more robust working hypotheses about resilience in urban and regional systems, taking into consideration all the facets of human life. Environmental aspects related to land use patterns and metabolic flows and the built environment should be integrated as well as social and economic dynamics and governance issues. With this in mind, the Resilience Alliance's research concept points in the right direction (Resilience Alliance, 2007).

A second weakness is related to the first. Despite a long chain of contributions concerning the meaning of urban resilience (e.g., Alberti et al., 2003; Vale & Campanella, 2005; Campanella, 2006; Ultamari & Rezende, 2007) there is still a lack of understanding concerning the processes and factors that make some cities and regions vulnerable and others resilient. This may in part be due to the extremely complex and open character of urban and regional social, economic, cultural, and political systems. Moreover, in systems where social and economic dynamics play a role, resilience has to incorporate many socio-economic aspects in a much more prominent way, such as human perception, behavior and interaction, as well as decision-making, governance, and the ability to anticipate and plan for the future. Simple analogies with ecological systems are therefore not always possible.

Finally, a third weakness is the lack of operationalization. There are many factors that affect a city's or a region's resilience. For example, a city or region with a robust, diversified economy, and good governance (among other factors), will rebound more quickly than a city or region with a narrowly specialized or weak economy (Campanella, 2006). Clear concepts to operationalize resilience for city and regional development are nonetheless rare.

One step in this direction has been undertaken by the *Building Resilient Regions Network* in the United States, where Foster (2006) differentiates between four types of criteria related to the assessment, readiness, response, and recovery capabilities of a region. She asks four overarching questions:

(a) How well can and does the region assess its vulnerabilities to disturbances and its capacity for responding to them?
(b) How well can and does the region ready itself to respond to assessments and potential disturbances?
(c) How effectively, in absolute and relative terms, does the region respond to actual disturbances?
(d) How effectively, in absolute and relative terms, does the region recover from the disturbance and learn from its lessons and insights?

Other organizations are on the same track. For example, the *Stockholm Resilience Centre* is looking for urban innovation in more concrete terms, and the *Association of European Schools of Planning*'s (AESOP) thematic group on 'Resilience and Risk Mitigation Strategies' is looking for new and more adequate planning approaches.

Despite the above-mentioned conceptual weaknesses, the discussion about resilience, and about urban and regional resilience in particular, demonstrates that we are not talking about just a dazzling term, although there is still a long way to go in the development of a constant concept to theoretically frame, analyze, and explain urban and regional resilience. In order to become more resilient, cities and regions "will need to adopt planning and design strategies that allow them to develop the capacities to better respond and adapt to the economic, social, and physical stresses they will face" (Newman, Beatley, & Boyer, 2009).

Dealing with Change in Germany – Steps towards More Resilience?

What does all this imply for a book about urban and regional resilience and for the way cities and regions deal with change in Germany? There are at least five aspects to consider:

First, we should keep in mind that the discussion about resilience is rather new in Germany. This means we have to draw insights from other fields of discussion such as sustainable urban and regional development.

Second, resilience research in Germany is still very much confined to natural disaster prevention, risk management, and adaptation strategies to climate change. Although these topics are of high relevance for urban and regional development, focusing on them alone would be by far too narrow an approach.

Third, we can learn from the international discussion that we should be very careful in applying the term 'resilience' to everything that is related to change towards more sustainable development. This would be by far too broad an approach. A distinction must be made between change and change management and resilience and resilience governance.

Fourth, in spatial research we should focus on the spatial dimension of resilience, and we should reflect on time and scale problems.

Fifth, we should be aware of the fact that disturbances are not automatically negative, and to be resilient is definitely more than being prepared for an unforeseen negative incident. To be resilient, means – in general terms – to be flexible enough to cope with disaster and decline, as well as to be able to make the best possible use of new opportunities which may either appear suddenly or develop over time.

Based on these considerations and taking the above-mentioned limitations into account, the 2010 edition of the German Annual of Spatial Research and Policy neither aims at giving a complete overview of resilience-related spatial research and practice in Germany nor tries to give a systematic overview of research findings. The objectives of this book are much more modest: The book sheds some light on recent resilience-oriented research by German scholars, which is mainly off the beaten track of natural hazards and climate change studies, and on support programs related to urban and regional resilience in Germany, even though they may not make an explicit reference to resilience in their terminology for the reasons described above.

The term resilience is understood here in a broad sense. It is not limited to natural hazards, risk reduction, climate change and more effective responses to them. In contrast, it includes strategies to prevent and recover from urban and regional distress and decline, and to cope with new social and economic challenges. Examples from different fields show how stakeholders in urban and regional development are dealing with change, or – as some of them would call it in the German context – attempting to become more sustainable.

The first two articles take a critical look at theoretical aspects of the concept of resilience as it is applied to issues of spatial development in an urban and regional context in Germany and in an international context. Thilo Lang (2010) provides insight into theoretical considerations regarding resilience and new institutional theory. Sonja Deppisch and Mareike Schaerffer (2010) take a critical look at the application of the concept of resilience with regard to large metropolitan areas. Like Robert Hassink (2010) in his recent article, they critically assess the resilience concept and its applicability. They conclude that the concept needs further development, i.e., especially when applied to large cities it should be able to address challenges of complexity in a more explicit way. Thilo Lang argues that a new institutional understanding of urban resilience may open up promising perspectives for social research about urban change.

Two articles deal with *German Federal Government* programs that are related to new challenges encountered in urban-regional development. Fabian Dosch and Lars Porsche (2010) describe ongoing activities to support cities and city regions in their efforts to achieve more resource efficiency. Three crucial issues are discussed: energy efficiency, adaptation to climate change, and resource-efficient land use management. Manfred Fuhrich and Evi Goderbauer (2010) deal with urban restructuring efforts in Germany. They describe two federal urban development programs in the eastern and western parts of the country (Stadtumbau Ost and Stadtumbau West). Both programs are individual attempts to provide modern responses to structural changes in Germany's society and economy. Although none of the authors use the term resilience to characterize the nature of the programs, they clearly demonstrate that more resilience-related work has been done in Germany than is conceptually expressed.

In their articles Joachim Burdack and Bastian Lange (2010) take a look at resilience in transition economies and the effects from a socio-economic point of view. They scrutinize the situation in post-transition cities in Central and Eastern Europe. They ask which "soft" and "hard" factors attract creative knowledge workers to metropolitan areas. Their conclusion is somewhat surprising and has severe policy implications. They recommend that policies should focus on retaining the creative autochthonous human capital and developing local talent instead of attempting to attract it from outside – endogenous development as an answer to "slow burn " effects.

Stephan Schmidt (2010) looks at the role of social capital as a means of increasing regional resilience. Using Switzerland as an example, he analyzes the country's New Regional Policy (Neue Regionalpolitik) and its orientation towards establishing learning regions. In order to foster regional innovation, a knowledge management system combining social capital and sustainable development has been designed. The author summarizes that this has considerably improved the ability of stakeholders to act. It has been a benefit for regional policy in general and can be viewed as a successful attempt to raise regional resilience.

Andreas Röhring and Ludger Gailing (2010) investigate the relationship between path dependency and resilience. They establish a link between the concept of resilience and the institutional approach of path dependency. Using the examples of two landscape regions in Eastern Germany, they argue that this link contributes to a better explanation of spatial development problems from a social science perspective. According to the authors, resilience cannot be reduced to ecological dimensions alone but should rather be seen as a socially constructed phenomenon. The ability to correct a given development path may be decisive in achieving resilience.

Thomas Naumann, Johannes Nikolowski, Sebastian Golz, and Reinhard Schinke (2010) deal with natural hazards. However, they take an engineering perspective and look at potential damage to buildings and ways to avoid it. Using the example of flood impacts, they present methods for analyzing and evaluating the vulnerability of buildings ex ante. Moreover, they deal with specific measures to reduce vulnerability and to increase the resilience of built structures. They understand these as being inherent aspects of modern risk management. The authors emphasize that the methodology as such is not confined to flooding but can easily be applied to other hazardous events, such as heavy rainstorms or heat waves.

Gérard Hutter (2010) also refers to natural hazards in his article. He is interested in mechanisms of planning for risk reduction and organizing for more resilience, as well as in ways to combine them. In line with his work in the thematic group of the *Association of European Schools of Planning* (AESOP) on 'Resilience and Risk Mitigation Strategies', he concludes that the context-specific dynamics of planning and resilience in organizations have often been overlooked, and need to be given more attention in both research and practice.

Heiderose Kilper and Torsten Thurmann (2010) argue that linking vulnerability and resilience research offers great potential for social science-oriented spatial research. They develop a series of questions for further research. They conclude that by employing theories originating from social sciences, a new understanding of the development of resilience as a "governance of preparedness" may evolve. They also stress the need to considerably broaden the thematic focus of vulnerability and resilience research beyond natural risks alone.

The final section of the book contains short reports on recent activities and projects in various parts of Germany. They give an insight into additional research and practice related to resilience and the reaction of cities and regions to change. Once again, these activities proove that there is much resilience-oriented work done in Germany that does not carry the term 'resilience' in its title.

The articles in this book show that at the present time urban regional resilience is neither a catchword nor a consistent concept for research and practice in Germany. They also demonstrate that more efforts are required to consolidate a resilience-related approach to spatial research and practice on regional and local levels. The articles presented here may be regarded as a contribution to this.

References

Alberti, M. & Marzluff, J. M. (2004). Ecological resilience in ecosystems: Linking urban patterns to human and ecological functions. *Urban Ecosystems, 7,* pp. 241-265.

Alberti, M., Marzluff, J. M., Shulenberger, E., Bradley, G., Ryan, C. & Zumbrunnen, C. (2003). Integrating Humans into Ecology: Opportunities and Challenges for Studying Urban Ecosystems. *BioScience, 53,* pp. 1169-1179.

Birkmann, J. (2008). Globaler Umweltwandel, Naturgefahren, Vulnerabilität und Katastrophenresilienz. Notwendigkeit der Perspektivenerweiterung in der Raumplanung. *Raumforschung und Raumordnung 66, (1),* pp. 5-22.

Berkes, F., Colding, J. & Folke, C. (2003). *Navigating Social-Ecological Systems – Building Resilience for Complexity and Change.* Cambridge: Cambridge University Press.

Brand, F. S. & Jax, K. (2007). Focusing the Meaning(s) of Resilience: Resilience as a Descriptive Concept and a Boundary Object. *Ecology and Society, 12(1),* p. 23.

Burdack, J. & Lange, B. (2010). Accomodating Creative Knowledge Workers? Empirical Evidence from Metropoles in Central and Eastern Europe (pp. 59-67). In B. Müller (ed.), *Urban Regional Resilience: How Do Cities and Regions Deal with Change?* Berlin/Heidelberg: Springer Verlag.

Campanella, T. (2006). Urban Resilience and the Recovery of New Orleans. *Journal of the American Planning Association, Spring 2006, 72,* p. 2.

Carpenter, S. R., Walker, B. H., Anderies, M. A. & Abel, N. A. (2001). From metaphor to measurement: resilience of what to what? *Ecosystem, 4,* pp. 765-781.

Christopherson, S., Michie, J. & Tyler, P. (2010). Regional resilience: theoretical and empirical perspectives. *Cambridge Journal of Regions, Economy and Society, 3(1).*

Crichton, D. (2007). What can cities do to increase resilience? *Philosophical Transactions of the Royal Society, 365,* pp. 2731-2739.

Cumming, G., Cumming, D. & Redman, C. (2006). Scale mismatches in social-ecological systems: causes, consequences, and solutions. *Ecology and Society, 11(1),* p. 14. Retrieved from: http://www.ecologyandsociety.org/vol11/iss1/art14/

Deppisch, S. & Schaerffer, M. (2010). Given the Complexity of Large Cities, Can Urban Resilience be Attained at All (pp. 25-34)? In B. Müller (ed.), *Urban Regional Resilience: How Do Cities and Regions Deal with Change?* Berlin/Heidelberg: Springer Verlag.

Dosch, F. & Porsche, L. (2010). Rebuild the City! Towards Resource-efficient Urban Structures through the Use of Energy Concepts, Adaptation to Climate Change, and Land Use Management (pp. 35-48). In B. Müller (ed.), *Urban Regional Resilience: How Do Cities and Regions Deal with Change?* Berlin/Heidelberg: Springer Verlag.

Duval, R. & Vogel, L. (2008). Economic Resilience to Shocks: The Role of Structural Policies. *OECD Economic Studies, (44), 2008.*

Fernández-Bilbao, A. & Twigger-Ross, C. (2009). Improving response, recovery and resilience. Improving institutional and social responses to flooding. *Science Report SC060019 – Work Package 2.* Bristol: Environment Agency.

Foley, J. A., DeFries, R., Asner, G. P., Barford, C., Bonan, G., Carpenter, S. R., Chapin, F. S., Coe, M. T., Daily, G. C., Gibbs, H. K., Helkowski, J. H., Holloway, T., Howard, E. A., Kucharik, C. J., Monfreda, C., Patz, J. A., Prentice, J. C., Ramankutty, N. & Snyder, P. K. (2005). Global consequences of land use. *Science, 309,* pp. 570-574.

Folke, C. (2006). Resilience: The emergence of a perspective for social-ecological systems analyses. *Global Environmental Change, 16,* pp. 253-267.

Folke, C., Colding, J. & Berkes, F. (2002). Building resilience for adaptive capacity in social-ecological systems. In F. Berkes, J. Colding & C. Folke (eds.), *Navigating Social-Ecological Systems: Building Resilience for Complexity and Change.* Cambridge: University Press Cambridge.

Foster, K. (2006). A case study approach to understanding regional resilience. Institute of Urban and Regional Development. Berkeley: University of California. Retrieved from: http://escholarship.org/uc/item/8tt02163

Foster, K. (n.d.). *Regional Resilience. How Do We Know It When We See It?* (forthcoming). Retrieved from: http://www.gwu.edu/~gwipp/Foster -- Regional Resilience May 2010.pdf

Fuhrich, M. & Goderbauer, E. (2010). Urban Restructuring – Making 'More' from 'Less' (pp. 49-58). In B. Müller (ed.), *Urban Regional Resilience: How Do Cities and Regions Deal with Change?* Berlin/Heidelberg: Springer Verlag.

Godschalk, D. R. (2003). Urban hazard mitigation: Creating resilient cities. *Natural Hazards Review, August 2003,* pp. 136-143.

Greiving, S. & Fleischhauer, M. (2009). Klimawandelgerechte Stadtentwicklung: Rolle der bestehenden städtebaulichen Leitbilder und Instrumente. *BBSR online publication, 24.*

Gunderson, L. & Holling, C. S. (2001). *Panarchy. Understanding Transformations in Human and Natural Systems.* Washington, DC: Island Press.

Hassink, R. (2010). Regional resilience: a promising concept to explain differences in regional economic adaptability? *Cambridge Journal of Regions, Economy and Society, 3(1),* pp. 45-58.

Holling, C. S. (1973). Resilience and Stability of Ecological Systems. *Annual Review of Ecology and Systematics, 4,* pp. 1-23.

Hutter, G. (2010). Planning for Risk Reduction and Organizing for Resilience in the Context of Natural Hazards (pp. 101-112). In B. Müller (ed.), *Urban Regional Resilience: How Do Cities and Regions Deal with Change?* Berlin/Heidelberg: Springer Verlag.

ICLEI (2010). Resilient Cities 2010. 1ˢᵗ World Congress on Cities and Adaptation to Climate Change. Retrieved from:
http://resilient-cities.iclei.org

Kates, R. W., Clark, W. C., Corell, R., Hall, J. M., Jaeger, C. C., Lowe, I., McCarthy, J. J., Schellnhuber, H. J., Bolin, B., Dickson, N. M., Faucheux, S., Gallopin, G. C., Grübler, A., Huntley, B., Jäger, J., Jodha, N. S., Kasperson, R. E., Mabogunje, A., Matson, P., Mooney, H., Moore III, B., O'Riordan, T. & Svedin, U. (2001). Sustainability science. *Science, 292,* pp. 641-642.

Kates, R. W. & Clark, W. C. (1996). Expecting the unexpected. *Environment, 38,* pp. 6-18.

Kilper, H. & Thurmann, T. (2010). Vulnerability and Resilience: A Topic for Spatial Research from a Social Science Perspective (pp. 113-120). In B. Müller (ed.), *Urban Regional Resilience: How Do Cities and Regions Deal with Change?* Berlin/Heidelberg: Springer Verlag.

Lang, T. (2010). Urban Resilience and New Institutional Theory – A Happy Couple for Urban and Regional Studies (pp. 15-24). In B. Müller (ed.), *Urban Regional Resilience: How Do Cities and Regions Deal with Change?* Berlin/Heidelberg: Springer Verlag.

Levin, S. A., Barrett, S., Aniyar, S., Baumol, W., Bliss, C., Bolin, B., Dasgupta, P., Ehrlich, P., Folke, C., Gren, I., Holling, C. S., Jansson, A., Jansson, B., Mäler, K. G., Martin, D., Perrings, C. & Sheshinski, E. (1998). Resilience in natural and socioeconomic systems. *Environment and Development Economics, 3,* pp. 221-235.

Lukesch, R., Payer, H. & Winkler-Rieder, W. (2010). Wie gehen Regionen mit Krisen um? Eine explorative Studie über die Resilienz von Regionen. *Studie im Auftrag des Bundeskanzleramtes Sektion IV, Abteilung 4, Raumplanung und Regionalpolitik.* Wien. Retrieved from: http://www.bundeskanzleramt.at

Müller, B., Finka, M. & Lintz, G. (ed.) (2005). *Rise and Decline of Industry in Central and Eastern Europe.* Berlin/Heidelberg: Springer Verlag.

Naumann, T., Nikolowski, J., Golz, S. & Schinke, R. (2010). Resilience and Resistance of Buildings and Built Structures to Flood Impacts – Approaches to Analysis and Evaluation (pp. 89-100). In B. Müller (ed.), *Urban Regional Resilience: How Do Cities and Regions Deal with Change?* Berlin/Heidelberg: Springer Verlag.

Newman, P., Beatley, T. & Boyer, H. (2009). *Resilient Cities. Responding to Peak Oil and Climate Change.* Washington D.C.: Island Press.

Pendall, R., Foster, K. & Cowell, M. (2010). Resilience and Regions: Building Understanding of the Metaphor. *Cambridge Journal of Regions, Economy and Society, 3(1),* pp. 71-84.

Perrings, C. (2002). *Lessons from Ecology. Discussion paper.* Retrieved from: http://www.york.ac.uk/depts/eeem/resource/perrings/

Resilience Alliance (2007). *Research Prospectus. A Resilience Alliance Initiative for Transitioning Urban Systems towards Sustainable Futures.* Retrieved from: http://www.resalliance.org/files/1172764197_urbanresilienceresearchprospect usv7feb07.pdf

Röhring, A. & Gailing, L. (2010). Path Dependency and Resilience – The Example of Landscape Regions (pp. 79-88). In B. Müller (ed.), *Urban Regional Resilience: How Do Cities and Regions Deal with Change?* Berlin/Heidelberg: Springer Verlag.

Schiappacasse, P. (n.d.). Urban Resilience as a sustainable framework to deal with the unforeseen – contributions from the urban planning perspective. Dresden (forthcoming).

Schmidt, S. (2010). A Strategy for Dealing with Change: Regional Development in Switzerland in the Context of Social Capital (pp. 69-78). In B. Müller (ed.), *Urban Regional Resilience: How Do Cities and Regions Deal with Change?* Berlin/Heidelberg: Springer Verlag.

Swedish Environmental Advisory Council (2009). *Resilience and Sustainable Development.* Retrieved from:
http://www.sou.gov.se/mvb/pdf/206497_Resilienc.pdf

The Resilient Region (2010). *Cambridge Journal of Regions, Economy and Society, 3(1).*

Ultramari, C. & Rezende, D. A. (2007). Urban resilience and slow motion disasters. *City & Time, 2(3),* p. 5.

Vale, L. & Campanella, T. (2005). *The Resilient City: How Modern Cities Recover from Disaster.* New York: Oxford University Press.

Walker, B., Holling, C. S., Carpenter, S. R. & Kinzing, A. (2004). Resilience, Adaptability and Transformability in social-ecological systems. *Ecology and Society, 9(2),* p. 5.

Urban Resilience and New Institutional Theory – A Happy Couple for Urban and Regional Studies?

Thilo Lang

1. Understanding Differences in Response to Urban Change

Every town and city is affected by trends of transformation and by processes of economic structural change. Some towns, cities, or regions can adapt to such developments while in others, structural change leads to multiple decline. The concept of urban resilience seems to offer ideas that make it easier to understand such differences.

Concerning the socio-economic impacts of the recent financial and economic crisis, there is no clear pattern which regions have been hit more severely than others by its impacts. Seemingly strong and shock-resistant cities such as London struggle in the light of an economic downswing as do more peripheral regions at the fringe of Europe. The current crisis has tended to lead decision makers to concentrate development impetus on large cities – continuing neoliberal development principles, expecting the rest of the country to profit from core-periphery spillover effects but instead further raising socio-spatial disparities (Weichhart, 2008; Krätke, 1995). Indeed, the contemporary tendency towards large globally networked city-regions combined with the turn towards neo-liberal policy measures in many European nations parallels widening gaps between sub-national regions, measured for example in income inequalities (Scott & Storper, 2003, p. 585).

Research about the response to urban decline is dominated by a strong governance perspective, highlighting the diffuse and multi-actor character of decision making that contrasts with state-centered hierarchical forms of government. Due to this shift from government to governance and due to an understanding of urban decline as being intensely related to normative perceptions and considerations of desirable and undesirable urban conditions, research about responses to decline often utilizes new institutionalist approaches. If we conceptualize urban resilience as a systemic capacity to cope with such challenges, which is inherent to the specific place under observation, we will have to link this to processes of and (institutional) frameworks for decision making instead of only focusing on structural determinants. Although places are specific and unrepeatable in their institutional environment, it is not 'the city' or 'the town' that acts but individual or collective actors. And it is their actions that constitute change. Hence, the underlying question for this paper is: How can the concept of resilience help researchers to study the response of local and regional actors to socio-economic challenges? To answer this question, I will at first explore

B. Müller, *German Annual of Spatial Research and Policy 2010*,
German Annual of Spatial Research and Policy,
DOI 10.1007/978-3-642-12785-4_2, © Springer-Verlag Berlin Heidelberg 2011

different understandings of urban resilience, secondly link this to concepts of urban governance and new institutionalism, and finally conclude with a brief judgment of the benefits and problems linked to the application of the resilience debate to studies about socio-economic urban change.

2. Understandings of Resilience

The debate about sustainable development and concerning the adaptation to climate change has introduced the idea of resilience to urban and regional studies on a broader basis. Discussions about urban vulnerability and resilience were also triggered in the context of some major urban threats and disasters in the last few years, in particular through the terrorist attacks in New York, the Asian tsunami and Hurricane Katrina in the New Orleans area. A German example is the Elbe flood in 2002, which had devastating effects on the city of Dresden in particular. From an urban planning perspective, Bosher and Coaffee (2008) deal with resilience as a capacity to avoid and manage such natural and human-induced hazards. Consequently, there is a strong link to debates of governance and there is also a strong political interest in supporting emergency preparedness – in particular in the UK[1].

There is more than one commonly agreed-upon concept of resilience in literature; across different disciplines resilience sometimes refers to contradictory characteristics (see also Medd & Marvin, 2005, pp. 45). Most resilience research is rooted in post-positivistic epistemology (cf. Walker et al., 2006) and applies system thinking, i.e., an understanding of the field of study as a complex multidimensional or hybrid system. Concepts of resilience are used to describe the relationship between the system under observation and externally induced disruption, stress, disturbance, or crisis. In a more general sense, resilience is about the stability of a system against interference. It is, however, more than a response to or coping with particular challenges. Resilience can be seen as a kind of systemic property.[2]

More recently there has been growing interest in the concept of resilience as a "concept for understanding, managing, and governing" (Walker, Anderies, Kinzig, & Ryan, 2006) complex social-ecological systems. Holling describes complex adaptive systems of people and nature as being self-organized with a few critical processes creating and maintaining this self-organization. Such systems of nature, humans, combined human-nature systems, or social-ecological systems can be perceived as being "interlinked in never-ending adaptive cycles of growth, accumulation, restructuring, and renewal" (Holling, 2001, p. 392). The accumulation and transformation of resources alternates with phases of creating opportunities

---

1   For more information see www.cabinetoffice.gov.uk/ukresilience.aspx and
     www.liveweb15.bham.ac.uk/index.shtml

2   Also in social psychology some scholars see resilience as being more than coping with
     critical events; it is "something underneath" (Murphy, 1974, p. 90, quoted in Welter-
     Enderlin, 2006, p. 10), it is the motivation of people that allows them to cope with critical
     events.

for innovation. Understanding these cycles, their temporal and spatial scales, as well as the relevant frames of reference would help to "identify the points at which a system is capable of accepting positive change and the points where it is vulnerable" (Holling, 2001, p. 392). In this context, (a) resilience as "a measure of its vulnerability to unexpected or unpredictable shocks" (Holling, 2001, p. 392), (b) internal controllability, and (c) the wealth of the system determining the range of possible future options are seen as the main properties shaping such adaptive cycles and the future state of the systems (Holling, 2001, pp. 393).

High resilience would allow for tests of novel combinations that trigger innovation and adaptation. This is particularly true if controllability is low and high resilience allows for the recombination of elements in the system because the costs of failure are low. However, in phases of vulnerability at multiple scales, revolutionary transformations are quite rare due to the nested character of sets of adaptive cycles. A combination of separate developments has to coincide, i.e., there is a need of re-combinations and inventions to occur simultaneously in order to open windows for creating fundamental new opportunity (Holling, 2001, p. 404).

Ideas of regional resilience can be linked to concepts such as learning regions, self-organization, innovative milieus, industrial districts, and some other strands of debate (see also Hudson, 2010, p. 12). Only a few scholars explicitly use the term resilience to investigate the response to urban and regional development problems (e.g., Hill, Wial, & Wolman, 2008; Gerst, Doms, & Daly, 2009; Hassink, 2010).[3] Important additional notions in this part of the literature are linked to equilibrium and path development. The topic under investigation is the way actors deal with external economic and social shocks. Economic resilience is seen as the capacity to address problems in a way that generates long-term success. This raises questions about the extent to which regions recover from underlying external shocks and re-establish their former states of equilibrium.

Empirical studies about these questions seem to be rare. Hill et al. quote two major studies in the US on the state level and the county/metropolitan level. The latter study indicates that areas with warm climates and those close to metropolitan cities showed the best post-shock recoveries (Feyrer, Sacerdote, & Stern, 2007, quoted in Hill et al, 2008, p. 5). Another study explored the different paths of development taken by urban IT centers in the US after the IT bust in 2000 (Gerst et al., 2009). Impacts of decline and paths of recovery varied considerably, demonstrating differences in regional economic resilience. Using quantitative methods, the research revealed that IT centers specializing in IT services performed better than those in manufacturing because of their highly educated labor force. Some centers even maintained growth due to their adjustment to changes in demand. The research, however, does not go into detail concerning the way these centers managed to adjust. Linked to questions of economic development, a system

---

3   In 2006, the US-based MacArthur Foundation established a research network entitled "Building Resilient Regions"
   (see http://www.macfound.org/site/c.lkLXJ8MQKrH/b.2617639 and
   http://brr.berkeley.edu/netobj.html).

perspective helps to shift the focus to the long-term structure of macroeconomic relationships and the relevant social, economic, and political institutions conditioning these structures (Hill et al., 2008, p. 2). Translated into economic development, studying resilience would involve studying the rise, stability, and decay of institutions conditioning long-term economic growth. Economic resilience would then be "the ability of a region [...] to recover successfully from shocks to its economy that either throw it off its growth path or have the potential" to do so (Hill et al., 2008, pp. 2).

3. Urban Governance, New Institutionalism, and Urban Resilience

There is a large body of literature chronicling the changing conditions of local decision making. Studies searching for the 'better' in urban governance, however, have mainly produced results highlighting problems and 'failures' instead of good practice and 'success' (for a summary see Lang, 2009, pp. 37). If governance is grounded in the empirical notion of a widening sphere of decision making, it cannot be limited to a heterarchical understanding nor to being automatically self-reflexive, self-organizing, innovative, or creative (such as promoted by, e.g., Kearns & Paddison, 2000, p. 847; Healey, 2004, p. 88; Jessop, 1998, p. 29; Rhodes, 1997, p. 53). Moving beyond the conflation of analytical claims and normative assumptions leads to an understanding of urban governance as an analytical dimension implying a view of organizations as much as processes, formal rules as much as informal practices, and the power of individual actors as much as the relevance of overall structures and specific local cultures.

Discussing ideas of complex adaptive systems and adaptive cycles within which resilience plays an important part (see above) shows stark overlaps with parts of the new institutional literature. Both 'schools of thought' discuss similar phenomena using a different scientific language. Adaptive cycles can be seen in the light of path-dependent developments (Pierson, 2000; North, 1990) and institutional thickness (Amin & Thrift, 1994) sometimes leading to functional, cognitive, or political lock-in (Grabher, 1993) hindering new forms of development. In such cases, the relevant system becomes maladaptive. North (1990) posed the question of how to avoid lock-ins and discussed the capacity to avoid lock-ins with the term, 'adaptation efficiency'. Holling (2001) suggested studying complex adaptive systems by looking at their inherent controlling processes, which are limited in number.

A new institutional research perspective could help to identify relevant controlling processes within an urban system under investigation. New institutionalism helps to understand relationships and processes in urban development policy (Lowndes, 2001) and opens up particular viewpoints on the formation of policy response to socio-economic challenges. Place and time-specific institutional environments function as a strong frame of reference. They are created as a result of earlier experiences and help structure local decision making-processes. In particular (collective or shared) norms, routines and practices constitute instituted forms of behavior which tends to make local policy and response to change path-dependent (Lang, 2009, pp. 58). Processes of governance must be seen as social processes that are shaped in a tense atmosphere of structure and agency. As decision makers are embedded in differing social and cultural structures (including different sets of institutions or multiple institutional environments) they "may have to choose among competing institutional loyalties as they act" (Peters, 1999, p. 26). Such selection processes depend on individual, collective, or organizational learning capacities based on the ability to learn from applied strategies and tactics in other contexts and at other times.

Understanding urban resilience only in terms of structural properties falls short under the precondition of a socially constructed world. If we perceive socio-economic resilience as being linked to those properties of the system that maintain the success and continuous existence of the system, new institutionalism could possibly help to focus research agendas in urban and regional studies. Combining the outlined new institutionalist positions with those from the resilience debate, we could see resilience as a systemic 'capacity', closely related to an institutional environment being supportive of the constant advancement of the system. Resilience could then be seen as being linked to a particular culture that constantly advances the key properties (or controlling processes) of the system. Elements of such institutional environments would favor experimentation, risk, and innovation in responding to external challenges and threats. For example, processes of decline in a particular industry with the related job losses could either be avoided or at least 'better' managed if the respective system could bear a high degree of resilience. Hence, the particular institutional environment would, for example, be supportive of foresight, developing advanced products, processes, or fields of economic activity in due time, and it would also allow for alternative futures in case particular paths of development came to an end. Such institutional environments will always be specific to place and time although they contain multi-level elements, i.e., in form of specific 'translations' of super-ordinated frameworks. An institutional understanding of resilience does not sustain ideas of a static set of properties. Resilience rather describes more or less elusive circumstances in the form of particular institutional practices and orientations which are supportive of an adaptation of the system. In this context it has to be kept in mind that resilience also risks being filled with normative expectations. Adaptation of the system, however, does not necessarily require being in line with broadly accepted 'positive' development trajectories.

4. Urban Areas as Complex Adaptive Systems

Perceiving urban areas as complex adaptive systems seems promising in developing research perspectives that better allow for an understanding of differences concerning the adaptability to socio-economic (and other forms of urban) problems. Research has shown that particularly when it comes to vulnerabilities at multiple scales, adaptation of the (urban) system to changing conditions is more than challenging (cf. Lang, 2009, pp. 28). So far, scholars have mainly offered suggestions about how to understand the problems such areas have in adapting, offering concepts such as institutional thickness or path dependency. However, understanding how change can be managed and how urban areas can adapt to altered framework conditions still remains an open question. Many scholars have concentrated their research on urban governance as an answer to urban problems. However, the understanding of governance is underpinned with normative notions about how governance should be rather than empirical findings. Instead, comparative governance research indicates that local regeneration strategies, emphasizing the creation of new forms of governance, are likely to fall short in terms of producing policy outcomes (Lang, 2009, pp. 192). Instead of perceiving urban governance as being innovative, self-organized, and inclusive, it should rather be seen as a predominantly incoherent amalgam of different networks and forms of collaboration of public, semi-public, and private actors, overlapping and diffusing at the same time.

New institutionalism also fails to offer a useful conceptualization of institutional change. Hence, the suggestion of understanding adaptation (which requires institutional change) as being related to nested adaptive cycles (see above) opens opportunities for advanced research and theory building in urban and regional studies. Related to old industrial regions, the idea of nested adaptive cycles helps to understand both the particularly serious problems of adaptation and slow recovery, and why it can nevertheless occur when a number of developments coincide to provoke fundamental system change.

For future research approaches concerning urban change, I would suggest combining the approach to urban areas as complex adaptive systems with some basic principles of new institutional theory in order to resolve some major problems of social science-based urban resilience research. Complex adaptive systems are seen as being self-organized, with a few critical processes creating and maintaining this self-organization. In particular, adaptive cycles linked to these controlling processes would be relevant to look at in the context of urban resilience research. The crucial question is how we can identify the processes which control the overall system. Literature concerning social-ecological systems does not say much regarding an answer to this question. In the context of urban, social, and economic development, new institutional theory can help to understand the institutional context in which such processes would take place. Indeed, Holling (2001, p. 404) formulates factors that would facilitate constructive change in a region under crisis conditions which are closely linked to locally specific institutional environments. Hill et al. (2008, p. 7) also suggest focusing research on institutional characteristics next to (strategic) private sector responses, governance response, and public policy actions.

The resilience debate in urban and regional studies also tends to seek particular local properties that make urban areas less vulnerable. Some literature raises expectations about self-contained urban systems functioning like a perpetual motion machine. This leaves aside the crucial question of national regulation and the necessity of investigating national forms of intervention.[4] Hudson thereby astutely discusses options for more resilient regions in relation to the resilience of capitalism and dominant neoliberal models of regional development which trigger national state interventions, and which have at best been partially and temporally successful in the past (Hudson, 2010). Indeed, neoliberal thought as a dominant feature of current capitalism can be seen as having become maladaptive, and as being a major threat to urban and regional resilience.

Due to being rooted in research about coping with extreme events, the concept of resilience has further major limitations when it comes to researching the urban response to social and economic challenges. Often questions about why and how external events are perceived as being a disturbance or crisis and about the intended state when these can be considered as being over are usually not included in research about resilience. Here, questions of power concerning the determination of what constitutes crisis and objectives for achievable adaptations are crucial and should be kept in mind (cf. Hudson, 2010, p. 13).

5.   Conclusions

A new institutional understanding of urban resilience opens up promising perspectives for social science research about urban change. Conceptualizing 'urban' as a complex multidimensional or hybrid system – system thinking is a key feature of resilience studies – leads us to look for the interaction of different dynamics and hybrid processes in their manifestation of vulnerability, crisis, and change. Such a system perspective seems suited to advance governance research, which is often overloaded with normative expectations of how governance should be. Conceptualizing 'urban areas' as complex systems does not allow for the general presumption that systems can be governed (Walker et al., 2006). I would rather argue that systems are per se not controllable. Systems are at best adaptive and self-organized.

The concept of resilience and the underlying theoretical body of knowledge could help to understand change in complex systems of spatial interdependencies, and thus fill a gap in institutional theory. On the other hand, by suggesting analytical categories, new institutional positions could help to identify the properties that make the urban system resilient. The understanding of development as being composed of nested adaptive cycles (Holling, 2001) thereby helps to understand change and persistence. In contrast to systems of urban governance, adaptive cycles can be seen as heterarchical and self-steering. Part of the conceptualization of adaptive cycles is that they only coincide with situations of multiple challenges in exceptional cases.

Social science attempts to conceptualize urban and regional resilience still need further advancement, in particular when it comes to questions of power, institutional

---

4   Empirical research shows the limited stabilizing capacity of local governance (Painter & Goodwin, 2000, p. 43) and the great importance of national factors when it comes to local forms of response to social and economic challenges (Lang, 2009, pp. 171).

constraint, and national regulation. It appears, however, promising to combine concepts of resilience and system thinking with new institutional ideas that fill these gaps. It is still an open question if and how change can be successfully managed. In the context of urban and regional development, this question is mostly linked to spatial and social justice and thus deserves more attention. The ideas presented in this paper may help to advance research concepts dealing with these issues.

References

Amin, A. & Thrift, N. (1994). Living in the global. In A. Amin & N. Thrift (eds.), *Globalization, Institutions and Regional Development in Europe* (pp. 1-22). Oxford: University Press.

Bosher, L. & Coaffee, N. (2008). Editorial: International perspectives on urban resilience. *Urban Design and Planning, 161, Issue DP4*, pp. 145-146.

Gerst, J., Doms, M. & Daly, M. C. (2009). Regional Growth and Resilience: Evidence from Urban IT Centers. *FRBSF Economic Review, 2009*, pp. 1-11.

Grabher, G. (1993). The weakness of strong ties: the lock-in of regional development in the Ruhr area. In G. Grabher (ed.), *The embedded firm: on the socio-economics of industrial networks* (pp. 255-277). London: Routledge.

Hassink, R. (2010). Regional resilience: a promising concept to explain differences in regional economic adaptability? *Cambridge Journal of Regions, Economy and Society, vol. 3, number 1*, pp. 45-58.

Healey, P. (2004). Creativity and Urban Governance. *Policy Studies, vol. 25, No 2*, pp. 87-102.

Hill, E., Wial, H. & Wolman, H. (2008). Exploring Regional Economic Resilience. *IURD Working Paper, 04*.

Holling, C. S. (2001). Understanding the Complexity of Economic, Ecological, and Social Systems. *Ecosystems, 4*, pp. 390-405.

Hudson, R. (2010). Resilient regions in an uncertain world: wishful thinking or a practical reality? *Cambridge Journal of Regions, Economy and Society, vol. 3, number 1*, pp. 11-25.

Jessop, B. (1998). The rise of governance and the risks of failure: the case of economic development. *International Social Science Journal, vol. 50, issue 155*, pp. 29-45.

Kearns, A. & Paddison, R. (2000). New Challenges for Urban Governance. *Urban Studies, Vol. 37, no. 5-6*, pp. 845-850.

Krätke, S. (1995). Globalisierung und Regionalisierung. *Geographische Zeitschrift, 83, book 4*, pp. 207-221.

Lang, T. (2009). *Institutional perspectives of local development in Germany and England: a comparative study about regeneration in old industrial towns experiencing decline.* Retrieved from: http://opus.kobv.de/ubp/volltexte/2009/3734/

Lowndes, V. (2001). Rescuing Aunt Sally: Taking Institutional Theory Seriously in Urban Politics. *Urban Studies, 38.11, October 2001*, pp. 1953-1971.

Medd, W. & Marvin, S. (2005). From the Politics of Urgency to the Governance of Preparedness: A Research Agenda on Urban Vulnerability. *Journal of Contingencies and Crisis Management, vol. 13, no. 2, June 2005*, pp. 44-49.

North, D. C. (1990). *Institutions, Institutional Change and Economic Performance.* Cambridge: Cambridge University Press.

Painter, J. & Goodwin, M. (2000). Local Governance After Fordism: A Regulationist Perspective. In G. Stoker (ed.), *The New Politics of British Local Governance* (pp. 33-53). Basingstoke: Palgrave Macmillan.

Peters, G. (1999). *Institutional Theory in Political Science: The 'New Institutionalism'*. London: Continnum.

Pierson, P. (2000). Increasing Returns, Path Dependence, and the Study of Politics. *American Political Science Review, 94, 2,* pp. 251-267.

Rhodes, R. A. W. (1997). *Understanding Governance: Policy Networks, Governance, Reflexivity and Accountability*. Buckingham: Open University Press.

Scott, A. & Storper, M. (2003). Regions, Globalization, Development. *Regional Studies, vol. 37, 6 & 7,* pp. 579-593.

Walker, B. H., Anderies, J. M., Kinzig, A. P. & Ryan, P. (2006). Exploring Resilience in Social-Ecological Systems through Comparative Studies and Theory Development: Introduction to the Special Issue. *Ecology and Society 11(1),* p. 12.

Weichhart, P. (2008). Neoliberalismus Meets Political Economy – Politikversagen, Entdemokratisierung und die vergebliche Hoffnung auf Governance in der Zweiten Moderne. In K. Bruckmeier & J. Serbser (eds.), *Ethik und Umweltpolitik: Humanökologische Positionen und Perspektiven* (pp. 213-236). München: pekom.

Welter-Enderlin, R. (2006). Einleitung: Resilienz aus der Sicht von Beratung und Therapie. In R. Welter-Enderlin & B. Hildebrand (eds.), *Resilienz – Gedeihen trotz widriger Umstände* (pp. 7-19). Heidelberg: Carl-Auer-Systeme.

Given the Complexity of Large Cities, Can Urban Resilience be Attained at All?

Sonja Deppisch, Mareike Schaerffer

1. Introduction

Large cities display an exceptional degree of complexity in a network of dynamic ecological, social, economic, cultural, and political interrelationships (Eckardt, 2009). They are characterized by high population density, high resource consumption as well as intensive land use, and they are often the origins of change processes. At the same time, large cities are particularly vulnerable to changes and disruptions because of the concentration of material assets and human lives. The concept of resilience describes the factors that can influence the ability of ecosystems and societies to withstand disturbances (Berkes & Folke, 1998; Folke et al., 2002; Walker & Salt, 2006). Empirical studies of resilience (e.g., Fleischhauer, 2008; Godschalk, 2003) often employ research approaches which focus on portions of the complex relationships between ecosystems and societies. The various dynamic relationships in large cities are difficult for existing research approaches to grasp in their entirety (Alessa, Kliskey, & Altaweel, 2009; Batty, Barros, & Alves, 2004; Eckart, 2009). In the following article, we will therefore discuss the question whether the existing concepts concerning urban resilience (Alessa et al., 2009; Fleischhauer, 2008; Godschalk, 2003; Hensta, Kovacs, McBean, & Sweeting, 2004) do justice to the complexity of large cities, using Hamburg and Istanbul as examples. The concepts found in research approaches on urban resilience will be confronted with characteristics of complexity. Finally, we will generate hypotheses about the question of to which extent the concept of urban resilience does justice to the complexity of large cities.

2. Complexity of Large Cities

2.1 Characteristics of Complex Cities

In light of the lack of a concrete, general theory of complexity, we will essentially refer to the 'topic of complexity' in the following article. The term is applied with reference to research on the development of complex systems which can be delineated vis-à-vis their surroundings out of individual elements as well as their emerging interaction (Manson & O'Sullivan, 2006). Here, emergence is taken to mean the result of synergies between system elements, going far beyond the mere

B. Müller, *German Annual of Spatial Research and Policy 2010*,
German Annual of Spatial Research and Policy,
DOI 10.1007/978-3-642-12785-4_3, © Springer-Verlag Berlin Heidelberg 2011

addition of individual system characteristics and components, and which is displayed in the development of a new structure or characteristic of the entire system (see, e.g., Gallagher & Appenzeller, 1999; Manson & O'Sullivan, 2006; Urry, 2005). Building on the results of chaos theory, namely that even small causes can trigger large effects and that the relationships between variables are not necessarily linear, non-linearity is an additional characteristic of the topic of complexity in addition to emergence (Urry, 2005; Eckardt, 2009). Furthermore, the aspect of time plays a central role in dealing with the topic of complexity. Time is considered as a variable, and as an internal trait of the system being observed, so time and space are viewed jointly and dynamically (Urry, 2005).

In particular cities with their various social, resource-based, and infrastructural networks are mentioned as examples of non-linearity and emergence. Complexity research, in turn, is mentioned as an appropriate means of being able to understand the real urban lifeworld. Existing urban research is hardly in a position to do so, due to its reduction of complexity (Allen, Strathern, & Baldwin, 2008; Eckardt, 2009). Complexity analyses do not use as a starting point an existing equilibrium that would be in place without the existence of humankind. Instead, the normal condition is to recover from the last crisis and to create new opportunities (Urry, 2005; Allen et al., 2008; Andersson, 2008). Because there is no equilibrium, it is difficult to model and anticipate the future, and attempts to do so are fraught with major uncertainties. Therefore, it is important to examine the history of the urban system more thoroughly in order to understand the form and output of the city (Andersson, 2008). In this context, when it comes to urban growth in particular, we point to self-reinforcing processes such as the development and further segregation of socially or even ethnically similar neighborhoods. The capability of guiding such processes as well as the interrelationships between social and ecological processes are relevant as well (Allen et al., 2008; Eckardt, 2009; Urry, 2005).

2.2 Two Examples: Hamburg and Istanbul

The general considerations can be illustrated using two large cities as examples: Hamburg and Istanbul. They are not compared with one another, but exemplify the elaborated characteristics of complex large cities. In the process, we refer back to existing published research results.

Istanbul displays both an intensive orientation to the West based on trade and economic relationships and a strong Ottoman character. As early as the 17th century, the Ottoman organization of the city resulted in the development of definable urban neighborhoods that were self-organizing in terms of social, religious, and economic issues, and whose residents manifested themselves as political citizens (Eckardt, 2009). After all, Istanbul was not made the capital of the Kemalist republic because of its Ottoman character and because it was considered too Western. Within Turkey, the city is very attractive because of its economic growth. The enormous migration to the city has led to in the large illegal 'Gecekondu' settlements at the urban fringe which has increased Istanbul's population by half a million year by year (Karaman,

2008; Radberger, 2001). In these urban quarters, it is striking that both economic activity and the settlements are illegal while at the same time they function as power bases for political parties, which in turn has effects nationally. Moreover, the uncontrolled processes of growth and urbanization lead to adverse impacts on environmental resources extending far beyond the local scale, as well as to social and cultural conflicts between the resident population and rural migrants (Eckart, 2009; Özcevik & Aysan, 2001; Radberger, 2001). Increased reintegration into the global economy, which raised the amount of capital in the city, furthermore triggered processes of gentrification which displaced especially the poor population to the city's surroundings and redefined the stable fabric of the old city neighborhoods, especially in the inner city (Karaman, 2008; Özcevik & Aysan, 2001).

In Hamburg too, processes of immigration, social closure, and segregation can be observed, processes through which certain lifestyle groups leave their marks on individual urban quarters and urban neighborhood cultures (Hentz & Strantzen, 1992). Processes of gentrification crowd out socially weaker groups of the population to the affordable suburbs. The results are increased commuter traffic, more regional sprawl, and a growing social disintegration in the city's core (Winkler, 2007). At the same time, Hamburg has been integrated in the global economy since it developed into a Hanseatic city and later became a leading seaport. The port in the city's center affects not only economic growth and the labor market, but also the city's spatial development, in particular the development of residential urban neighborhoods close to the center, which results above all in new conflicts between diverging land use interests (FHH, 2003; Schubert, 2009). The development of the city of Hamburg and its port and labor market is, in turn, integrated in various interrelationships with the continuing changes of the global economy, transport, environment, climate, and demography (cf. Niebuhr & Stiller, 2005; Schubert, 2009).

3. Urban Resilience against the Background of various Concepts of Resilience

What is urban resilience, and how do research approaches based on the term deal with complex large cities? This will be presented in the following article. Initial attempts to work with the concept of resilience refer to ecosystems and their capability to compensate for disturbances (Holling, 1973). In the social sciences and economics, resilience is also seen in the context of the ability of individuals, groups, and businesses to resist disturbances (e.g., Briguglio, Cordina, Farrugia, & Vella, 2006; Rutter, 1987). Concepts of social-ecological resilience which emphasize the interrelationships between ecosystems and society are increasingly being discussed (Adger, 2000; Berkes & Folke, 2003; Walker & Salt, 2006). Characteristics of resilient social-ecological systems include (a) the ability to absorb shocks and still remain within a given state, (b) the ability of self-organization, and (c) the capacity for learning and adaptation (Folke et al., 2002).

The social-ecological concept considers resilience to be the extent of tolerance that cities can muster in case of disturbances. Urban resilience is therefore linked to the ability to recover after shocks, and to reorganize by establishing new processes and structures (Campanella, 2006; Australian Commenwealth Scientific and Research Organisation [CSIRO], Arizona State University, & Stockholm University, 2007; Folke et al., 2002). Existing approaches point to the complex relationships between ecosystems and various forms of land use on the part of urban society, between different levels of action, and with additional underlying conditions (Colding, 2007; Walker & Salt, 2005). The natural settings of cities and concentrations of material assets affect their vulnerability to disturbances. The dynamic social, economic, and political interactions within urban societies as well as with other subregions and political levels are relevant as well (Füssel & Klein, 2006). Both the physical and the social systems influence a city's sensitivity (Godschalk, 2003). Approaches to promote adaptive capacity are discussed and developed for various partial areas of social life in order to understand processes that could render cities resilient (CSIRO et al., 2007; Folke et al., 2002). Empirical works on social-ecological and urban resilience (e.g., Alessa et al., 2009; Colding, 2007; Fleischhauer, 2008; Godschalk, 2003; Hensta et al., 2004) make recommendations for the appropriate scope of studies. Alessa et al. (2009) propose a typology of resilient settlements which combines the inherent robustness of natural resources, social organizations, infrastructures, and technologies. In interlinking various factors of resilience, the authors turn away from systematizing approaches, rather emphasizing the disordered and chaotic dimensions of social-ecological systems. The typology is connected with indicators such as diversity, collectivism, and variability. If the majority of indicators scores high, a spatial entity is considered to be resilient (Alessa et al., 2009). According to Godschalk (2003), a system is resilient when confronted with catastrophes if principles such as redundancy, diversity, efficiency, autonomy, collaboration and adaptability are present. Hensta et al. (2004) base their work on this approach. Nonetheless, they make either the physical or the social system a separate topic of discussion. Colding (2007) and Fleischhauer (2007) focus on the physical and ecological areas of a city by considering the significance of planning and land use. As a consequence, the approaches assess only partial systems, e.g., a city's infrastructure (e.g., Fleischhauer, 2008), or social (social capital or organizational structures) and physical aspects (building structures), by employing characteristics such as diversity, robustness, or capacity to learn independently of one another (e.g., Godschalk, 2003). Therefore, they offer answers relating only to the aspects of the complex interactive urban structure that were studied.

4.   Urban Resilience in Complex Large Cities

The studies on urban resilience mentioned above largely confirm our initial hypothesis that the currently existing research approaches to urban resilience do not do justice to the topic of complexity in a comprehensive manner. It is true that the basic concepts of urban resilience and the complexity of large cities are similar, as they assume dynamic interactions between city, environment, and society. Although many research approaches to urban resilience do simplify after all, not least in order to be able to classify (e.g., Alessa et al., 2009), the topic of complexity necessarily requires observation of the criteria emergence, non-linearity, and the dynamics of time and space. Taking account of the demonstrated complexity criteria in research approaches to urban resilience would require observing the ecological and social subsystems jointly. This requirement is already formulated in the concept of social-ecological resilience, but empirical research approaches rarely fulfill it. Alessa et al. (2009), for instance, attempt to develop a complex research approach, but they themselves consider it to be provisional and simplified. With reference to the criteria of complexity it has to be recognized that initial prerequisites for empirical studies on 'more complicated' resilient social-ecological systems are met. However, it nonetheless remains debatable to what extent precisely a typology is helpful for studying urban resilience in complex large cities, or whether such a typology cannot be considered helpful as it does not produce results going beyond a classification.

Using 'diversity' as an indicator employed by various authors (Alessa et al., 2009; Godschalk, 2003) for urban resilience, we discuss in the following article to what extent the existing concepts take these interactions into account. For example, diversity in social systems is linked to social capital, cultural integration, or diverse value systems (Alessa et al., 2009; Godschalk, 2003). Diversity in ecological or physical systems, on the other hand, might stand for polycentric settlement patterns or varied physical structures (Fleischhauer, 2008). Concerning emergence, non-linearity, and space-time dynamics in Istanbul and Hamburg, interactions become apparent that can be grasped only rudimentarily if nothing but a combination of the parameter social capital or settlement patterns is employed. In Istanbul, the indicator 'diversity' must involve the variety of value orientations, their influence on organizational forms, as well as urban neighborhoods with interplay emerging in many ways. In Hamburg, the multitude of lifestyle groups has formed various settlement structures and urban neighborhood cultures which are to be taken into account in their many dynamic interrelationships. It becomes apparent in this respect that models of urban resilience should link not only ecological and social parts of the city but also diversity and other principles (e.g., adaptability).

In the approaches studied, however, these linkages are not made. Instead, they are added (Fleischhauer, 2008; Godschalk, 2003; Hensta et al., 2004), or the decision is made to focus only on individual aspects (e.g., Colding, 2007). On the one hand, principles such as diversity, robustness, and redundancy are then applied to the institutional structures. Organizational forms, social networks, and value systems play a role here. On the other hand, building structures, infrastructures, supply and waste management structures as physical systems are studied separately from social factors (Godschalk, 2003). Applied in this way, the concept of urban resilience with its currently debated research approaches does justice to the complexity of large cities only rudimentarily. Overcoming the separation between the living and the built urban worlds and transcending the study of parts of the city (Dangschat

& Hamedinger, 2007; Eckardt, 2009) is difficult to implement, especially for the applied models. Although Alessa et al. (2009) point out that the complexity of urban systems is not taken into account sufficiently in the approaches to urban resilience, they do not entirely bridge the gap separating the individual parts. In their typology, they combine social and ecological developments. But when evaluating the settlement types, they again examine partial aspects such as social capital or government organizations.

Going beyond this coherent social-ecological examination – inasmuch as, once it has been developed further, it will be applicable for empirical work and not only for manageable research designs – taking the topic of complexity into account should have much more far-reaching consequences even beginning with the research approach. A different, that is, broadened way of thinking is considered to be necessary. This approach would have to address the manifold processes and elements in large cities jointly, in the ways they depend on each other and interact, instead of studying them piece by piece and dividing them into individual elements, periods of time, or levels. Broadening the approaches used to date by referring back to strategies developed in the social sciences and the humanities appears to be a possibility. For example, the method of dense qualitative case descriptions of individual cities could be helpful. This method employs historical material and historical-critical analysis of written sources (Jordan, 2008). The case descriptions could then be followed by hermeneutic procedures (Gadamer, 1965). Hence, it appears necessary to expand the number of disciplines involved in studying urban resilience in order to include these strategies and methods in a field that has to date been approached especially from the perspectives of environmental and hazard research.

5.   Conclusion and Outlook

The concept of urban resilience is used to describe characteristics and potentials of cities and urban societies to react to disturbances and processes of change as flexibly and robustly as possible. Research approaches that study the resilience of cities have referred to individual partial systems, problem areas, and particular institutions to date. But large cities in particular are distinguished by their complexity. Emergence, non-linearity, and dynamics of time and space are characteristics that draw attention to the manifold interconnections of effects both in cities and between cities and their surroundings. Using Hamburg and Istanbul as examples, the dynamics of global conditions as well as their interplay with local emerging processes of urban development becomes apparent. Furthermore, many interconnections between historical, economic, sociocultural, political, and ecological developments are relevant. A simplification and reduction to partial aspects in order to grasp complex relationships does not appear reasonable. The concept of urban resilience and the corresponding research approaches in their current form do justice to the complexity of large cities only rudimentarily. The concept of urban resilience pursues a very ambitious goal that seems practically unattainable because of the complex interconnections between the city, the environment, and society. With reference to the research approach, the concept of urban resilience must confront the challenges of complexity explicitly when it is applied to complex large cities and must be developed further in this respect.

References

Adger, W. N. (2000). Social and ecological resilience: are they related? *Progress in Human Geography, 24(3),* pp. 347-364.

Alessa, L., Kliskey, A. & Altaweel, M. (2009). Towards a typology for social-ecological systems. *Sustainability: Science, Practice and Policy, 5(1),* pp. 31-41.

Allen, P. M., Strathern, M. & Baldwin, J. (2008). Complexity: the integrating framework for models of urban and regional systems. In S. Albeverio et al. (eds.), *The dynamics of complex urban systems: an interdisciplinary approach* (pp. 21-41). Heidelberg: Physica.

Andersson, C. (2008). Ontogeny and Ontology in complex systems modeling. In S. Albeverio et al. (eds.), *The dynamics of complex urban systems: an interdisciplinary approach* (pp. 43-58). Heidelberg: Physica

Australian Commenwealth Scientific and Research Organisation [CSIRO], Arizona State University & Stockholm University (2007). *Urban Resilience Research Prospectus: A Resilience Alliance initiative for transitioning urban systems towards sustainable futures.* Retrieved from: http://www.resalliance.org/files/1172764197 urbanresilienceresearchprospectus v7feb07.pdf

Batty, M., Barros, J. & Alves Junior, S. (2004). Cities: Continuity, Transformation, and Emergence. *CASA Working Paper Series, 72.*

Berkes, F. & Folke, C. (1998) (eds.). *Linking Social and Ecological Systems. Management Practices and Social Mechanisms for Building Resilience.* Cambridge: Cambridge University Press.

Briguglio, L., Cordina, G., Farrugia, N. & Vella, S. (2006). Conceptualising and Measuring Economic Resilience. In L. Briguglio, G. Cordina & E. Kisanga (eds.), *Building the Economic Resilience of Small States* (pp. 265-288). Malta: Islands and Small States Institute.

Campanella, T. (2006). Urban Resilience and the Recovery of New Orleans. *Journal of the American Planning Association, 72(2),* pp. 141-146.

Colding, J. (2007). Ecological land-use complementation for building resilience in urban ecosystems. *Landscape and Urban Planning, 81,* pp. 46-55.

Dangschat, J. S. & Hamedinger, A. (2007): Sozial differenzierte Räume – Erkenntnisinteresse, Problemlagen und Steuerung. In J. S. Dangschat & A. Hamedinger (eds.), *Lebensstile, Soziale Lagen und Siedlungsstrukturen. Forschungs- und Sitzungsberichte der Akademie für Raumforschung und Landesplanung, Volume 230.* Hanover: Verlag der ARL.

Eckart, F. (2009). *Die komplexe Stadt. Orientierungen im urbanen Labyrinth.* Wiesbaden: VS Verlag.

FHH – Freie und Hansestadt Hamburg (2005). *Sprung über die Elbe.* Hamburg.

Fleischhauer, M. (2008). The role of spatial planning in strengthening urban resilience. In H. J. Pasman & I. A. Kirillov (eds.), *Resilience of Cities to Terrorist and other Threats* (pp. 273-298). Dordrecht: Springer.

Folke, C., Carpenter, S., Elmqvist, T., Gunderson, L., Holling, C. S. & Walker, B. (2002). Resilience and Sustainable Development: Building Adaptive Capacity in a World of Transformations. *Ambio, 31(5),* pp. 437-440.

Füssel, H.-M. & Klein, R. (2006). Climate Change Vulnerability Assessments: An Evolution of Conceptual Thinking. *Climate Change, 75(3),* pp. 301-329.

Gadamer, H.-G. (1965). Wahrheit und Methode. Grundzüge einer philosophischen Hermeneutik (2nd ed.). Mohr: Tübingen.

Gallagher, R. & Appenzeller, T. (1999). Beyond reductionism. *Science, 284(5411),* pp. 79-80.

Godschalk, D. R. (2003). Urban Hazard Mitigation: Creating Resilient Cities. *Natural Hazards Review, 4(3),* pp. 136-143.

Hensta, D., Kovacs, P., McBean, G. & Sweeting, R. (2004). *Background Paper on Disaster Resilient Cities.* Ottawa: Institute for Catastrophic Loss Reduction.

Hentz, S. & Strantzen, B. (1992). *Kulturkomplex.* Hamburg: Stadtteilkultur in Hamburg.

Holling, C. S. (2003). Foreword: The backloop to sustainability. In F. Berkes, J. Colding & C. Folke (eds.), *Navigating social-ecological systems.* Cambridge: Cambridge University Press.

Holling, C. S. (1973). Resilience and Stability of Ecological Systems. *Annual Review of Ecology and Systematics, 4,* pp. 1-23.

Jordan, S. (2009). *Theorien und Methoden der Geschichstwissenschaft.* Paderborn: Schöningh.

Karaman, O. (2008). Urban Pulse – (Re)Making Space for Globalization in Istanbul. *Urban Geography, 29,* pp. 518-525.

Manson, S. & O'Sullivan, D. (2006). Complexity theory in the study of space and place. *Environment and Planning, A 38,* pp. 677-692.

Niebuhr, A. & Stiller, S. (2005). Demographischer Wandel und Arbeitsmärkte in Norddeutschland. *Wirtschaftsdienst, 5,* pp. 326-332.

Özcevik, Ö. G. & Aysan, M. (2001). A clustering evaluation of the Istanbul peri-urban areas. *Trialog, 70,* pp. 34-39.

Radberger, R. (2001). *Monitoring der Verstädterung im Großraum Istanbul mit den Methoden der Fernerkundung und der Versuch einer räumlich-statistischen Modellierung.* Göttingen: Georg-August Universität.

Rutter, M. (1987). Psychosocial resilience and protective mechanisms. *American Journal of Orthopsychiatry, 57,* pp. 316-331.

Schubert, D. (2009). Stürmische Zeiten für die nordwestdeutschen Seehafenstädte. *RaumPlanung, 14,* pp. 199-204.

Urry, J. (2005). The complexity turn. *Theory, Culture & Society, 22(5),* pp. 1-14.

Walker, B. & Salt, D. (2006). *Resilience Thinking: Sustaining Ecosystems and People in a Changing World.* Washington D.C.: Island Press.

Winkler, M. (2007). Flächensparsame Siedlungsentwicklung – ein „nachhaltig" verfolgtes Ziel? Eine Zwischenbilanz am Beispiel der Metropolregionen Hamburg und Wien. *RaumPlanung, 132(3),* pp. 119-124.

Rebuild the City! Towards Resource-efficient Urban Structures through the Use of Energy Concepts, Adaptation to Climate Change, and Land Use Management

Fabian Dosch, Lars Porsche

1. The Challenge of Resource-efficient Urban Development

More and more people live in cities. Within the context of the energy crisis, climate change, and demographic change, one of the greatest challenges is the resource-efficient conversion of urban regions. The level of new housing construction is presently a great deal less than one percent of existing buildings. Current and future urban development will mainly involve existing structures. 'Rebuild the City!' is the mission. When the challenges of climate and resource-efficient urban development are taken into consideration, this becomes much more complex than merely building new structures.

Fig. 1: Urban Development through the recycling of brownfields. Source: Dosch (2003).

B. Müller, *German Annual of Spatial Research and Policy 2010*,
German Annual of Spatial Research and Policy,
DOI 10.1007/978-3-642-12785-4_4, © Springer-Verlag Berlin Heidelberg 2011

Cities and urban living contribute significantly to resource consumption and CO_2 emissions (Breheny, 1992). At the same time they also offer a high potential for the efficient use of limited resources due to population density.

More than two-thirds of the world's population live in urban regions, and four-fifths of all jobs are located there. The absolute consumption of power there is accordingly high in comparison to peripheral areas.

Three aspects that have been treated in a rather solitary fashion up to now with regards to urban development, i.e., energy, climate, and land use, require an integrated approach in the context of these challenges. Firstly, through the use of renewable resources and an increase in energy efficiency, a simultaneous contribution to climate protection can be made. Secondly, by using the necessary climate adaptation measures, an increased demand for areas which are derelict but usable can be generated. And thirdly, in a best-case scenario, synergies can be created due to the use of brownfields and recycled land, or through the dual utilization of existing land, buildings, and areas adjacent to buildings.

Resource-efficient urban development aims to:

- Promote urban development that has balanced density; area revitalization up to site recycling management that has a high degree of area productivity,
- Expand post-fossil fuel mobility,
- Extensively promote resource and energy-efficient construction and the use of renewable energy sources,
- Focus on an environmentally sound development structure that promotes elderly and family-oriented general services, the further development of urban cultural landscapes, and agriculture close to urban areas.

The challenges of ensuring resource-efficient urban development and renewal are great. Active and integrated strategies are called for in order to maintain cities as attractive areas in which to live and work. This requires that the relationship between urban development and the saving of resources be restored. Significant factors in this are economical land management and space-saving infrastructure concepts (mobility, supply and disposal, etc.). The question of a suitable model also has to be raised.

Because their populations are so densely concentrated, cities have a considerable potential to reduce CO_2 emissions. And due to the growing quantity of recycled land within them, they have areas which are unused or could be dually used; meaning the potential for generating renewable energy is also high. This potential needs to be systematically taken advantage of and used in energy and climate concepts. Because cities in particular are affected by climate change, a key challenge lies in the environmentally friendly conversion of the existing built environment. Efficiency in both energy and land use have to go hand in hand in future urban development, as both serve to improve climate protection. Climate adaptation also requires (open) space if individual measures are to be implemented.

Key policy guidelines exist for all of the areas of resource-efficient urban development mentioned here, i.e., for energy efficiency, climate protection, and

Fig. 2: New open space – Westpark Bochum. Source: Dosch (2008).

land management. In 2007 The *German Federal Government* developed goals at the national level in its 'Integrated Energy and Climate Protection Concept' (IEKP) in order to counter challenges posed by developments on the global energy market (especially oil and gas prices) and by climate change. Regarding climate, the *European Commission* published a White Paper entitled 'Adapting to Climate Change: Towards a European Framework for Action' (COM, 2009). *The German Federal Government* laid the cornerstone for a medium-term process prior to this with its 'German Strategy for Adaptation to Climate Change' (DAS) (Bundesregierung, 2008). The goal is to reduce vulnerability to the effects of climate change, maintain and increase the adaptability of natural, social, and economic systems, and to take advantage of any possible opportunities. In order to implement adaptation strategy an action plan adjustment in 2011 is foreseen. In terms of land management policy, the goal remains to significantly reduce the amount of land used for development. Energy efficiency, climate protection, and land use management will also be given a high priority in the 17th *German Federal Government*'s coalition treaty.

The attainment of political goals and the carrying out of necessary scientific analyses with their resulting gains in knowledge can only occur if regional and municipal levels are involved in the process. Concrete measures can only be developed, agreed upon, and implemented at these levels. The *German Federal Institute for Research on Building, Regional Affairs and Spatial Development* (BBSR) has attempted to maintain a balancing act between experimental and model projects in its research. All of their investigations, the approaches and results of which are briefly described in this article, are based on the following premise: Resource-efficient urban development has the goal of reducing both the burden on the environment and overall costs through a more efficient and economical use of natural resources.

2.   Energy-efficient Urban Development and Renewal

Energy forms the basis of urban life and economic development. During the past 100 years cities have largely moved away from the recycling of materials and circular land use management. They now rely on a largely regional supply of external resources and disposal of resultant waste materials. Since oil prices peaked in July 2008, the exogenous conditions of energy supply have been more incalculable, and the market more erratic and less predictable. The awareness of the finite nature of fossil energy sources is growing. Gas imports, from Eastern Europe for example, are also limited and are a politically sensitive issue as well. On political and various planning levels new approaches and solutions to finding a source of energy that is sustainable, secure, and as climate-neutral as possible are being demanded.

But how can urban areas make an effective contribution through energy-related building renovation and the increased use of renewable energy, such as combined heat and power (CHP)?

The focus is on climate change-proof urban development and on how this can be successful. Within the context of energy conservation, increasing energy efficiency, and renewable energy, the urban planning, technical, and economic aspects of urban development need to be combined in the areas of mobility and transport, new construction and existing buildings, and settlement development. The starting point is the integration of energy issues in a long-term process of urban planning and urban redevelopment as well as in the planning of energy supply. The objective is to create integrated, strategically oriented long-term urban development, urban renewal, energy savings, environmental improvement, a socially responsible and secure energy supply, and economic development (cf. BBSR, 2010a). Contributions urban and spatial development can make to energy efficiency and energy supply are mainly in the area of existing structures: The avoidance of energy consumption as well as an efficient supply of energy within a community or city through the use of appropriate infrastructure. Potential areas of activity are especially the reduction of energy use in existing buildings through an increase in thermal insulation, and an improvement in the efficiency of decentralized systems in buildings through the increased use of regenerative forms of energy and the establishment of local energy concepts (Koziol & Porsche, 2008). Two examples illustrate the potential constraints and opportunities, i.e., the renovation of buildings and the use of renewable forms of energy.

The generation of heat accounts for around 40 percent of Germany's total energy consumption, and of this, 85 percent is used for heating and hot water in private households (BMVBS, 2007). Opportunities arising from considerations of energy efficiency are not always compatible with current urban development. From an energy-point of view buildings constructed during the 'Gründerzeit' (approximately 1890-1910) have a high energy demand per person. Energy-related renovation is costly, and yet the urban and architectural value of these buildings, as well as the quality of living they offer, is beyond question. This example shows that the merging of contrasting objectives requires a multidisciplinary discussion of urban development policy. In the future it will certainly prove useful to complement tried and tested integrated urban development concepts with aspects of climate change-proof urban development.

Potential exists not only in the restoration of buildings, but in the production of renewable energy. In principle, urban areas are also capable of producing some of the energy (electricity and heat) they need themselves. A study carried out by the *German Federal Ministry of Transport, Building and Urban Affairs* (BMVBS) as part of the 'Experimental Housing and Urban Development' (ExWoSt) research program entitled 'The Use of Urban Open Space to Generate Renewable Energy' aimed at the creation of a coherent strategy for presenting the total potential of renewable energy, i.e., all possible applicable technologies within a city. This is where the unique and little-studied potential for untapped 'usable energy areas' is found, for example brownfields, conversion sites, vacant lots, and areas held in reserve, as well as roofs and building façades and the subsurface surrounding buildings (e.g., geothermal). The study showed that even in densely populated urban areas like Gelsenkirchen land, i.e., space, for the generation of energy was available. 897 hectares in the city could be used in a neutral fashion. This represents a heat gain of 1,650 Gigawatt hours (GWh) per year and 667 GWh per year of electricity (BMVBS/BBSR, 2009). Appropriate methods can thus be developed, for example to support and accelerate the use of renewable sources of energy in urban areas. This would also be a sensible and, if necessary, temporary use of urban open space, especially of brownfields and recycled areas, or roofs and façades (Grimski & Dosch, 2010). Up to now studies have concentrated more on individual energy sources, such as the potential of solar energy. The study reveals that an integrated approach is possible and necessary.

The use of renewable energies in built environments requires a new mindset, as well as action by the population, network operators, and energy suppliers. On the one hand a new type of infrastructure is required, one that ensures a locally controlled supply of renewable energy (from small producers as well), for instance through pooling in virtual power plants. On the other hand the use of renewable energy will lead to a changed cityscape, which in turn requires a rethink as well as acceptance by the population of the urban compatibility of such measures. Power plants that generate renewable energy will be considered incompatible if they influence the cityscape and compatible if they are not visible. By contrast, geothermal probes, the use of ambient air, geothermal energy, and hydropower have a very small effect on the urban landscape.

The field of action with regard to energy-based urban renewal is diverse and complex. Scientific studies will allow for solutions to be developed that will in turn

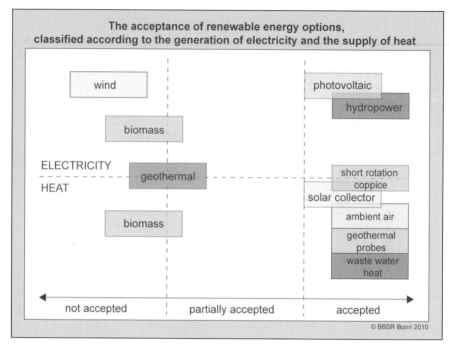

Fig. 3: The acceptance of renewable energy options in urban areas. Source: BMVBS (2009).

enable cities and communities to successfully deal with this complexity and develop strategic measures. Examples of this include energy concepts that complement urban development concepts and identify needs, potentials, and constraints that can be synchronized with climate adaptation measures.

3.   Urban Development Adapted to Climate Change

Cities are especially affected by climate change. Climate change increases the existing problem of urban heat islands even more. The consequences are, among other things, significantly higher temperatures, longer periods of heat, increased cooling requirements, reduced thermal comfort, and a rising demand for water. Extreme events such as the flooding of rivers, heat waves, and intense heavy rainfalls also become more common, endangering residents and causing damage to the built environment. Gradual changes in amounts of runoff or the level of groundwater, etc. can bring about new demands on existing buildings and infrastructure, for example on drainage systems and transport routes.

Individual indicators determined in climate models, for example the number of very hot days (cf. BBSR, 2010b), or aggregated indicators of potential impacts, for example active complexes of heat stress (cf. BBR, 2008, pp. 11), indicate particularly high levels in agglomerations in the southwest and southeast of Germany. This is confirmed by smaller-scale working models based on a grid for heat stress using statistical models (for example the weather-based regionalization method WETTREG), for instance the heat index with the UBA (Federal Environment Agency) technical information system 'Climate Change and Adaptation FISKA' (GIS-based information system for adaptation strategies in Germany). In a current pilot project micro-scale investigations are being used to look into, among other things, thermal stress at the neighborhood level (www.klimaexwost.de).

Changes in annual precipitation and in extreme weather conditions cannot be modelled as well as temperatures. Trends found in ensemble simulations, however, indicate a significant increase in the number and duration of extreme weather conditions in urban areas.

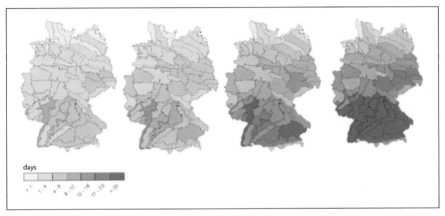

Fig. 4: Number of hot days in a comparison of the periods 1961-1990, 2011-2040, 2041-2070, 2071-2100. Projection. Results from the climate model REMO (run in 2008) using the example of hot days for scenario A1B. Source: BBSR (2010b).

The result: Cities must begin to prepare themselves for climate change now due to the persistence of the built environment. The challenge lies in an environmentally friendly restructuring of existing settlements and in settlement structure adaptation measures. In doing so, vulnerabilities (for a definition see BBSR et al., 2009, pp. 17) need to be determined using specific urban and regional procedures. In pilot projects vulnerability indicators were determined using GIS; for instance by overlaying heat stress with the development of the population over 65 years old, or in more complex approaches with social vulnerability, for example (cf. www.klimamoro.de). In a total of eight pilot projects, 'Spatial Strategies for Climate Change' (KlimaMORO), i.e., regionally specific concrete action plans for climate adaptation, will be developed by 2011. A preliminary study (BBSR, 2010b) was used to prepare the way by making:

- A spatial typing of the regional vulnerability (exposure, potential impacts, and sensitivity) to climate change,
- A nationwide analysis of spatial planning tools and governance approaches,

- The development of specific regional management, mitigation, and adaptation strategies as part of regional planning; a product of this is the development of key objectives within a regional ideal-typical framework of action entitled 'Climate Adaptation', i.e., a so-called 'blueprint' (BBSR, 2009b).

Just as on the regional level, local climate policies are also challenged in two ways: climate protection as the avoidance of emissions and adaptation to climate change. A specific urban and regional combination of strategies is required, as is consultation concerning sectoral policies. In the absence of technical planning for climate change, urban and spatial planning can take on a coordinating role and promote concrete measures for resilient spatial structures that are adapted to climate change: for instance, through the use of fresh air corridors, extensive open space areas as cold islands, the prevention of additional soil sealing, and the moderate climate-compatible densification of urban structures.

In general, the strategies of climate change-proof urban development can be illustrated as follows (cf. BBSR, 2009c):
- Identification of the risks vulnerabilities pose with regard to climate impacts,
- Strategies for dealing with uncertainties,
- Actor and government-based strategies: 'climate-proof planning', risk management approaches,
- Material strategies: energy-efficient construction, thermal insulation in existing buildings,
- Structural strategies: decentralized concentration, mixed use, circular land use management, green networks,
- Functional strategies: traffic control systems, development of renewable energy,
- Institutional strategies: intercommunal cooperation in infrastructure development, agreement on CO_2 reduction targets.

In the KlimaExWoSt 'Urban Concepts for Climate Change', the main research area 'Municipal Strategies and Potentials' has nine pilot projects in which 'Municipal Action Plans Climate Change' will develop resilient and thus climate change-proof spatial structures by 2012. The objectives are to identify cross-sector vulnerabilities, the development of a decision support system (DSS), and the development of concrete but easily transferable adaptation measures in an intersectoral dialogue. In the preliminary study 'Climate Change-proof Urban Development – Meeting Causes and Effects of Climate Change with Urban Concepts' the range of tasks of climate change-proof urban development was drawn up and published in five expertises: the performance potential and range of tasks of urban development (cf. BBSR, 2009a), the impacts of climate change, overall concepts and instruments, planning practice, and climate-proof planning.

The main product of the ExWoSt preliminary study is a decision support system for integrated urban action concepts for climate protection and adaptation to changes. It was developed as an independent actor-based consultancy tool for the concrete implementation of measures and will be successively expanded upon and linked with other assistance tools (www.stadtklimalotse.net). Using a specific selection mask, which also differentiates between the size of communities, it will be possible to select from among 138 measures in 10 fields of activity according to classified criteria such as cost-relevant measures, etc. These are linked to hundreds of references to legal texts at the federal level as well as to a huge number of national and international best practices and concepts.

Interim results of both aforementioned fields of research and their pilot projects (KlimaMORO and KlimaExWoSt) led to the first contributions to the DAS's Action Plan Adaptation with regard to transferable products, methods, procedures, and concepts. In carrying out the pilot project, a technically and conceptually more intensive exchange about climate-relevant projects and programs is being conducted, especially within the *Federal Ministry of Education and Research*'s (BMBF) funding programs 'KLIMZUG' and 'klimazwei', as well as in over 30 INTERREG IV B projects dealing with the subject of climate and various departmental research projects. Adaptation is a common learning process (BMVBS/BBSR, 2010).

4. Resource-efficient Land Use Management with Site Recycling Management

Dispersed settlement patterns represent an inefficient use of land. Since 2002 attempts have been undertaken to reduce the consumption of land for traffic areas and settlements to 30 hectares per day in Germany by 2020. The main control variable of resource-efficient urban development is land use management, achieved

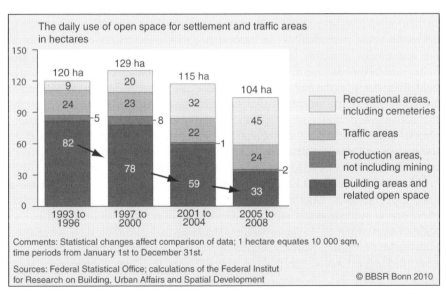

Fig. 5: The daily use of open space for settlements and traffic areas 1993-2008. Source: Ferber, Grimski, Glöckner, and Dosch (2010).

through, among other things, site monitoring, recording the amount of available land, increased urban inner zone development and renewal of the existing stock, site recycling and increased funding, economic incentives, and quantity control measures within regional planning. In the past few years five major amendments to the Building Code have been made, and are aimed at urban inner zone development and a renewal of the existing stock, especially through the now well-known 'accelerated procedure' for the development of urban areas in accordance with paragraph 13 of the Building Code (BauGB). Compared to 2000, the consumption of land for settlements and traffic areas is declining, and was approximately 104 hectares per day between 2005 and 2008, particularly for buildings and open space.

The main reason for the decline in the amount of land consumed is a strong decline in overall construction. Nevertheless, the density of settlements continues to decrease due to the continued consumption of land and stagnating population growth, which has led to the inefficient utilization of settlement infrastructure. There is a large and growing potential for long-term unused areas in existing settlements. This large potential of available land for urban development should be used again for reasons of resource-efficiency, and also for interim uses and renaturalization. New ways and procedures for reuse must be developed to this end (cf. BBSR, 2010c).

Many projects within the funding programs 'Research for the Reduction of Land Consumption and for Sustainable Land Management' (REFINA) as well as 'Land-use in a Cycle' focus on the development and testing of measures to prevent the consumption of land and promote site recycling. As part of the ExWoSt research program 'Circular Land Use Management in Cities and Urban Regions' (2004-2007) more than 50 new and existing instruments were systematized. Using simulation games these instruments were tested for the contribution they made to achieving goals, practicability, and acceptance in five model regions. As a result, the instruments available today allow for a rapid entry into circular land use management, for example through the use of an integrated framework for action. In field trials, funds for the mobilization of small-scale brownfields, implementation of a levy on earmarking greenfield sites for development, and integrated frameworks for action were preferred (cf. http://www.flaeche-im-kreis.de/english_version. phtml). At the same time, the problems of land consumption need to become more transparent and predictable in order to increase awareness of them. To this end, cost-benefit calculators have been developed by REFINA.

As a result of the REFINA program findings, cost transparency became a main task (Preuss & Floeting, 2009). Great importance was placed on improved coordination at the regional level, good examples of practice, and communication with a target group of decision-makers. Deciding to fund urban development on brownfields or existing building land as opposed to the development of greenfields goes hand in hand with a gain in the quality of life by linking economic, ecological, and social goals.

5. Conclusion

Urban development is going through a period of change – especially with regard to existing built areas. This should also be seen in the context of continuing demographic change. Energy and land use efficiency, as well as climate adaptation measures, have to go hand in hand with urban development in order to be able to recognize conflicting demands for land at an early stage and to make synergies possible. There is no alternative to resource-efficient urban development, and its aim must be to use natural resources more efficiently and economically in order to use them in a more productive and cost-saving way. The premise has to be that the decline in the consumption of resources is absolute, i.e., 'rebound effects' due to the increased consumption of less expensive resources will be avoided (FWU, 2009).

This is where a great opportunity exists to take advantage of synergies created from urban planning, economic, ecological, and social demands. That success is possible is shown by the approaches depicted in the fields of energy, climate, and land use, which now have to be integrated. An economic, efficient, environmentally friendly, and socially just, i.e., sustainable, supply of energy for cities has to be the primary political goal of urban development. In the context of dwindling fossil fuels and increasing energy costs, urban structures and ways of life have to be designed in an energy-efficient and climatically-adapted way. Especially in light

Fig. 6: A Plus Energy House. Source: Dosch (2009).

of an increasing use of renewable energy, regional relationships between urban and rural communities need to be encouraged.

There is no alternative to a vision of a compact and dense city. Urban open space will certainly need to be adjusted with regard to energy usage and densities that are adapted to climate change.

Spatial planning can (further) develop adequate planning and design processes using appropriate settlement patterns: High-quality dense building areas, energetically renovated urban quarters, new housing and commercial development with low energy, zero energy, plus energy, and passive energy standards, consumer-oriented mobility options, a custom power generation and supply infrastructure, and environmentally friendly compensation (i.e., open space) areas adjacent to housing and places of work. Climate and energy adaptation concepts also need to be established as part of urban development.

The implementation of these ambitious climate and energy goals is especially common at local, municipal, and regional levels. Support is vital as integrated urban development and climate and energy concepts are developed and implemented, as otherwise fragmented and uncoordinated measures will be the most common result. Current programs for the renovation of buildings, energy efficiency, and the use of electricity and heat from renewable sources of energy in Germany are having an impact. Dealing with spatial structures should be an obligatory part of all funding measures. Instruments for identifying and implementing measures on municipal and local levels are also necessary, such as energy and climate adaptation concepts as part of urban development concepts. The pilot projects of ExWoSt and the spatial planning pilot project MORO show how concrete integrated action plans and measures for resource and energy-efficient urban development that is adapted to climate change, as well as practical recommendations for politicians and actors, can be developed.

References

Breheny, M. J. (1992). *Sustainable Development and Urban Form*. London: Pion.
BBR – Bundesamt für Bauwesen und Raumordnung (ed.) (2008). Raumentwicklungsstrategien zum Klimawandel – Vorstudie für Modellvorhaben. *BBR online publication, 19/08.*
BBSR – Bundesinstitut für Bau-, Stadt- und Raumforschung (2010a). *Energetische Stadterneuerung*. Retrieved from: www.energetische-stadterneuerung.de
BBSR – Bundesinstitut für Bau-, Stadt- und Raumforschung (ed.) (2010b). Klimawandel als Handlungsfeld der Raumordnung: Ergebnisse der Vorstudie zu den Modellvorhaben „Raumentwicklungsstrategien zum Klimawandel". *BBSR Reihe Forschungen, issue 144,* p. 122.
BBSR – Bundesinstitut für Bau-, Stadt- und Raumforschung (2010c). Neue Zugänge zum Flächenrecycling. *Informationen zur Raumentwicklung, book 1/2010.*
BBSR – Bundesinstitut für Bau-, Stadt- und Raumforschung (ed.) (2009a). Klimawandelgerechte Stadtentwicklung. *BBSR online publication, 22/09.*
BBSR – Bundesinstitut für Bau-, Stadt- und Raumforschung (ed.) (2009b). Entwurf eines regionalen Handlungs- und Aktionsrahmens Klimaanpassung („Blaupause"). *BBSR online publication, 17/09.*
BBSR – Bundesinstitut für Bau-, Stadt- und Raumforschung (ed.) (2009c). Klimawandelgerechte Stadtentwicklung – Wirkfolgen des Klimawandels. Skizzierung einer klimawandelgerechten Stadtentwicklung. *BBSR online publication, 23/09.*
BMBF – Bundesministerium für Bildung und Forschung (2010). *REFINA – Forschung für die Reduzierung der Flächeninanspruchnahme und ein nachhaltiges Flächenmanagement.* Retrieved from: www.refina-info.de
BMVBS – Bundesministerium für Verkehr, Bau und Stadtentwicklung (ed.) (2009). *Nutzung städtischer Freiflächen für erneuerbare Energien.* Special publication.
BMVBS/BBSR (eds.) (2010). *2. MORO-Konferenz „Raumentwicklungsstrategien zum Klimawandel".*
BMVBS/BBSR (eds.) (2007). CO_2-*Gebäudereport 2007.*
Bundesregierung (2008). *Combating Climate Change. The German Adaptation Strategy.* Berlin: BMV.
Bundesregierung (2007). *Bericht zur Umsetzung der in der Kabinettsklausur am 23./24. August 2007 in Meseberg beschlossenen Eckpunkte für ein Integriertes Energie- und Klimaprogramm, IEKP.*
COM – European Commission (2009). *Adapting to climate change: Towards a European framework for action. COM 147.* Brussels.
Dosch, F. & Porsche, L. (2009). Ressourcenschonende Stadtentwicklung. Nachhaltige Siedlungsstrukturen durch Energiekonzepte, Klimaschutz und Flächeneffizienz. *Informationen zur Raumentwicklung, book 3/4,* pp. 255-271.

Everding, D. (ed.) (2007). *Solarer Städtebau. Vom Pilotprojekt zum planerischen Leitbild.* Stuttgart: Kohlhammer.

Ferber, U., Grimski, D., Glöckner, S. & Dosch, F. (2010). Stadtbrachenpotenziale: Von Leuchttürmen und Patchwork. *Informationen zur Raumentwicklung, 1/2010*, pp. 1-11.

FWU (ed.) (2009). Nachhaltiges Wachstum. *Wissenschaft & Umwelt Interdisziplinär, No. 13.* Vienna: Forum Wissenschaft und Umwelt.

Grimski, D. & Dosch, F. (2010). Brownfield management in Germany – a sustainable issue. *Journal of Urban Regeneration and Renewal, Vol. 3, Number 3*, pp. 246-262.

Koziol, M. & Porsche, L. (2008). Innovative Konzepte und Modellvorhaben der Weiterentwicklung kommunaler technischer Infrastruktur – Das Beispiel der energetischen Stadterneuerung. *Die Zukunft der städtischen Infrastrukturen. Deutsche Zeitschrift für Kommunalwissenschaften, vol. II/2008*, pp. 97-116.

Preuß, T. & Floeting, H. (eds.) (2009). *Folgekosten der Siedlungsentwicklung. Bewertungsansätze, Modelle und Werkzeuge der Kosten-Nutzen-Betrachtung.* Berlin: Difu.

Urban Restructuring – Making 'More' from 'Less'

Manfred Fuhrich, Evi Goderbauer

1. Restructuring of Cities – A Long-term Task

The restructuring of our cities has developed into an important area of urban development policy in recent years. Governmental urban restructuring programs in eastern and western Germany face entirely different challenges than former urban renewal programs in West German cities. In the early years of urban development grants, the issue was first of all to eliminate 'unhealthy living conditions' and to overcome 'functional weaknesses' in formally designated urban renewal areas. This occurred against the background of continuous economic growth and unchecked sprawl – and older, pre-World War II neighborhoods were neglected as a result (Zapf, 1969).

1.1 Rescuing the Older Neighborhoods – An Urban Development Challenge in East and West

The conference "Rettet unsere Städte jetzt!" ("Save our cities now!") was the trigger for society to recognize the value of the building stock once more (Deutscher Städtetag, 1971). In East Germany, the focus was on expanding built-up areas, as this was the only way to reach the goal of solving the housing question. Here, too, a growth-oriented policy resulted in the older neighborhoods being neglected. It was not least the demands to rescue the older neighborhoods that led to increasing social discontent, which in turn brought about the collapse of the social system of the *German Democratic Republic* (GDR).

Even today, the issue is still the future of the building stock in German cities, albeit in different contexts and intensities in eastern and western parts of the country. The radical economic downturn in the new federal states left considerable industrial and commercial brownfields behind, a result of companies closing down. And due to increased unemployment and migration from this region, the number of vacant residential buildings rose to more than one million (BMVBS, 2007).

In order to interpret this figure, we need to take into account the fact that the GDR 'contributed' approximately 400,000 vacant apartments in pre-World War II buildings to the country's unification, vacant because they were uninhabitable. Suburbanization, which set in after unification in many places, and the pent-up

B. Müller, *German Annual of Spatial Research and Policy 2010*,
German Annual of Spatial Research and Policy,
DOI 10.1007/978-3-642-12785-4_5, © Springer-Verlag Berlin Heidelberg 2011

demand for single-family homes exacerbated this situation. By now, more than 270,000 apartments have been torn down. Nonetheless, the results of an initial evaluation demonstrate that an additional 220,000 will be vacant in the next few years in the absence of demolition (BMVBS, 2008).

1.2 Urban Restructuring in the New Federal States – Demolition and Enhancing Neighborhoods as a Dual Strategy

The urban development program 'Urban Restructuring in the New Federal States' (Stadtumbau-Ost), financed by the federal government and the federal states, began as early as 2002, featuring two program components which were given fundamentally the same weight: demolitions and measures to enhance urban neighborhoods. In the initial years, the public considered the program mainly a countrywide demolition program. Tearing down prefabricated residential buildings at the city's edge has slowed down in the meantime, and the focus has shifted to enhancing older neighborhoods within the urban fabric. In many places, considerable progress can be seen. Measures in 410 municipalities totaling 2.5 billion euros of public funds have been carried out to date. The federal states have concentrated on very different aspects in selecting and implementing projects.

The program Stadtumbau-Ost is increasingly becoming similar to urban renewal as it was practiced for decades in West Germany. With one major difference, however: besides modernizing housing and enhancing residential areas within the fabric of the city, the task is above all to dispose of apartments which will not meet demand in the long term and to adapt urban infrastructure, as the next wave of population decline in the eastern Germany can already be foreseen.

1.3 Urban Restructuring in the Old Federal States – From Urban Renewal to Urban Restructuring

In the West, the phenomenon of a decline in population, also called 'shrinkage' in short, was foreseeable as early as the 1980s, and was taken up in professional debates (Häußermann & Siebel, 1988). Population figures could be kept constant only with high levels of immigration from abroad. In fact, in addition to a gradual change in the structure of the population, it was possible to foresee a continual loss of population for many cities and towns. This did not materialize, or not as seriously, as expected; migration within Germany after unification at least overshadowed this structural development so that many affected cities no longer considered the problem to be grave.

Today, the problem is increasingly becoming recognizable in western German cities, too, and is in fact being recognized in the realm of politics. Individual cities have established an 'ombudsperson for demography'. Nonetheless, the pressure to act is currently not as high as in the eastern German cities. The gradual change

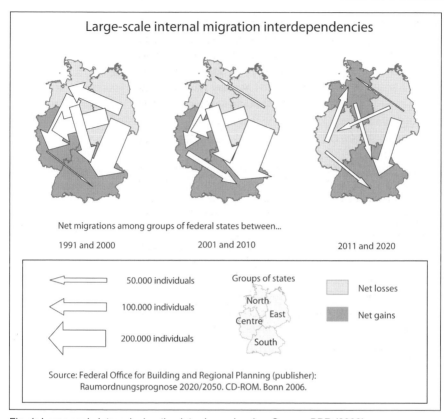

Fig. 1: Large-scale internal migration interdependencies. Source: BBR (2006).

holds the opportunity to face the new challenges strategically and to take preventive measures. The lack of drama in western Germany, however, invites people to push the issue aside. The abstract topic 'demography' is increasingly the subject of attention, and the consequences at the local level are becoming more and more apparent in the western Germany as well. However, vacant housing is more dispersed in these areas. Consequentially, the program area 'Stadtumbau-West' has less of a focus on demolishing residential buildings. Instead, the challenges of urban development without growth are at the center of attention, characterized not only by a declining population, but also by the spatial consequences of crises in certain industries (Fuhrich & Kaltenbrunner, 2005).

1.4 Pilot Projects in Western Germany – A Reflection of Industries in a Global Crisis

The first pilot projects in the program 'Stadtumbau-West' within the framework of the program 'Experimental Housing and Urban Development' (ExWoSt) were located in cities affected by the demise of certain industries, e.g., shipbuilding, production of textiles, shoes, and porcelain as well as fisheries. But traditional military towns are increasingly affected by shrinkage as well. In contrast to urban renewal, the task in shrinking cities and towns is no longer only strengthening functions and modernization, but changing or abandoning functions. Individual cities and towns must be reinvented; in this way, old industrialized cities and towns are transformed into high-value service and knowledge centers. Examples of such development include the 'Science Center Dynamikum' in Pirmasens or the 'Saarterrassen' in Saarbrücken. While the former emerged from the restructuring of the Rheinberger factory complex, which used to be the center of shoe production in Germany, the latter is the successful reuse of a former steelworks site to a location for new media and telecommunications businesses.

In individual areas, these developments are just beginning, in others, they have not yet been completed. It is certain that the challenges will increase, as well as the uncertainties. For neighborhoods undergoing transformation, there are no panaceas or guarantees concerning their future perspectives for use. Service centers, too, are subject to increasing global competition. In addition, people are realizing that urban development without growth will be the normal state of affairs for urban development policies in the future. This applies to traditional economic centers as well, where growth and decline are taking place at the same time and in neighboring locations. In other words, it is not only crisis-ridden urban regions that are affected by shrinkage, but increasingly many parts of Germany.

1.5 New Challenges for Eastern and Western Germany

The question arises for both eastern and western areas of the country how quality can be enhanced while quantity is reduced. Beyond highly-publicized lighthouse projects, two challenges for sustainable urban development arise in particular: interim use and renaturation. Both strategies prove to be unaccustomed options. Existing building and planning law is tailored to this challenge only insufficiently, and the actors, too, are still learning how to handle temporary uses or even abandoning a land use, that is, giving up settled areas for the long term. These strategies, however, will be of increasing importance for sustainable urban development policy in the future.

2.   Interim Use

2.1 Interim Use as a Planning Strategy

Cities and towns in the process of urban restructuring are characterized by vacancy. This problem affects municipalities to different degrees, depending on how the economic and demographic structural crises play out. When handling vacant properties, the municipalities tend to use building and land management geared toward existing stock more than in the past, but for many, the search for appropriate uses or users for the vacant real estate is proving very difficult. In order to keep options for using existing areas or buildings open for the future of the municipality, thinking strategically in terms of interim solutions, permitting interim uses, and planning for them as far as possible can be a reasonable approach. The following aspects can guide a municipality's actions in this regard:

- Interim use temporarily enhances the urban development quality compared to the existing situation of vacancies,
- Interim use supports the following use or prepares for it strategically,
- Interim use proves to be an appropriate use for the site and itself develops into a long-term solution.

In other words, interim uses can play a role wherever the pressure to use real estate or the demand for immediate and long-term following uses is too low, but where it is not yet necessary to give up the site once and for all. Using sites temporarily can be tolerated from an urban development perspective, or can even be desired in terms of urban planning strategy. After all, interim uses often grow out of citizens' involvement or a creative milieu which can also provide positive impulses in the discourse about developing particular sites.

2.2 Diversity of Sites and of Types of Interim Uses

Overall, interim uses gain relevance in cases where use of more land and buildings is discontinued than can be reused in the short-term. In the context of urban restructuring, interim use projects have successfully been realized in very different settings of vacant real estate, and this continues to be the case (Schlegelmilch, 2009). The spectrum of sites ranges from disused industrial, military, and infrastructure sites to land formerly occupied by residential high-rises now demolished and vacant plots within the urban fabric, storefronts, big box retail outlets, and residential and office buildings. The various sites, however, with a variety of underlying conditions, are suited for different kinds of interim uses which in turn are just as diverse. Projects from the fields of the arts, culture, and events are to be found here, as well as business start-ups, smaller shops and markets, and city beach clubs. Many interim use projects are sports and recreational facilities such as exercise rooms, artificial beaches on vacant land, playgrounds, and space for various trendy sports. Temporary plantings and allotment gardens on vacant lots and formerly built-up sites serve recreational purposes as well as enhancing open space. One form of interim use on large pieces of disused land that has been tested only in a few cases is the generation of renewable energy, for example short-rotation plantations or photovoltaic installations established for a limited period of time (BMVBS/BBSR, 2009a). These examples do not cover the full range of types of interim uses, for it is precisely their temporary nature that attracts 'spatial pioneers' who enjoy experimenting with new ideas for uses (BMVBS/BBR, 2004).

2.3 Obstacles and Limitations to Interim Uses

Problems in implementing interim uses often begin when the various actors interact, because the municipality, the proprietor of the real estate in question, and the interim user do not always pursue the same goals or have the same interests. The interim users – individuals, associations, citizens' initiatives, or small business owners – are seeking low-cost space available short-term with little red tape for their (at times) unconventional ideas for land use, and are willing to accept uncertain prospects or invest their own labor in return. The municipality may be interested in vitalization of the site and enhancing its image, but also seeks to ensure the legality of the project. The proprietor would like to have as little work as possible managing the property, would like to prevent vandalism and dilapidation, and would like to achieve at least a small amount of income. Operating costs and building costs are to be cut, or to be borne by the interim users. The proprietor's fear that the interim users will stay on the property, standing in the way of the desired long-term following use, may reduce the proprietor's willingness to permit the interim use. Those involved are not always aware of the contractual possibilities available for handling such situations. Whether or not an official permit can be issued for a land use often depends on the extent to which exceptional circumstances qualify the interim use as acceptable. Concepts for clearing the property, which include unequivocal rules for the phase ending the interim use, can help create such circumstances. For an interim use is especially successful if it is in fact a limited use, and if it paves the way for a long-term use of the land or the building (BMVBS/BBR, 2008).

As there is no shortage of available and vacant real estate during urban restructuring, interim uses will continue to play a major role here. The growing need for expert advice arises not only in terms of initiating and implementing projects, but also regarding arrangements for terminating an interim use. This need has resulted in the establishment of municipal agencies or private brokers in individual towns in Germany (BMVBS/BBR, 2008). Some municipal administrations also manage property pools with buildings available for interim uses. Such activities fundamentally confirm the strategic importance that will continue to be granted the topic of interim use in urban restructuring in order to secure sustainable urban structures.

3. Renaturation

3.1 Renaturation as a Forward Strategy

Urban development in Germany is characterized to an ever stronger degree by the simultaneity of growth and shrinkage and their spatial proximity to one another (Fuhrich, 2003). In the case of lacking long-term perspectives for reusing buildings – especially after large-scale demolition – the option to systematically enhance an area by means of following renaturation measures appears to be of increasing importance. In 85 percent of the urban restructuring measures in the context of

'Stadtumbau-Ost', the following use does not involve buildings (BMVBS, 2007). But the strategy of giving up built-up areas large-scale still encounters mental and financial limits. There is a need to clarify issues, especially regarding planning and building law, conditions for government support, and the consequences of value adjustments for businesses when land uses are given up (Baumgartner & Seidl, 2004).

Especially in the case of large tracts of derelict land, particularly at the edge of the city, using the land for forestry and agriculture has proven to be more cost-effective than open space and recreational areas, which require more upkeep. Proximity to nature gained in this way can contribute to enhancing the value of the previously derelict site. These new qualities of disused land can be employed as strategies to counter ongoing suburbanization. However, long-term successes cannot be achieved by means of isolated individual measures. It is impossible to simply "switch on" (Le Roy, 1983) nature. Rather, coordinated concepts, which are to counter 'natural' and unguided dissolution of the urban fabric, are to be developed as balanced strategies for urban development policy. The debate is rarely about pure forms, i.e., forests, agriculture, or open spaces. Instead, the locally specific combination of very diverse land-use options is dominant. This entails conflicts between different interests, but in the long term, it makes land use more stable thanks to flexible elements (Giseke, 2007).

3.2 Revision of Traditional Patterns of Thinking

Renaturation of settled land requires us to revise our ingrained ways of thinking. Giving back settled land is a 'radical' step that cuts to the chase of the familiar land use (Becker & Giseke, 2004). Giving up a previous land use always means experiencing a loss. The insight that the accustomed no longer exists and the future cannot yet be experienced proves to be a mental challenge at the threshold "no longer – not yet" (Baumgartner & Seidl, 2004). It is easier to take up this challenge when advantages are apparent. This applies all the more if the state of uncertainty of the unattractive derelict land or vacant buildings lasts for a longer time after the previous use has been abandoned, if the site is becoming dilapidated or security problems arise. Renaturation is successful if 'going back' can also be explained as 'going forward'. In other words, it is decisive to communicate the loss as a gain. A lack of open space within the urban fabric or adverse climate conditions, for example, can be used as arguments for viewing renaturation as positive in the long term.

Giving up a land use once and for all is neither abstract nor 'purely spatial'. It also has concrete financial ramifications. Real estate prices decrease as soon as demand in the local market declines. Value adjustments must be made due to a lack of opportunities for exploitation. This results in a poorer credit rating for the owner because of a lack of collateral. Costs for maintaining the building while meeting the requirements to secure public safety and to avert danger must be considered.

In light of these costs, and if the property generates no income, it stands to reason that proprietors will tend to end their responsibility and give up their dilapidated property in hopeless cases (BMVBS/BBSR, 2009b).

3.3 Renaturation as a Logical Response to Shrinking

Renaturation projects are the most logical response to structural change in our cities. New urban landscapes are not isolated objects planted in existing urban structures or catastrophic perforations as the result of processes of erosion. Instead, they are closely linked with other urban land uses in spatial and functional terms. New green corridors or 'oases' are not to be considered opposites to the city, but as urban elements within the urban fabric. Viewing the city as an organism helps us to understand the essential, vital function of green lungs (Heiland, 2006).

Small measures can trigger large effects in built-up areas. Demolishing individual buildings or small blocks triggers both tangible progress in terms of the microclimate and enhances the quality of the directly surrounding area, which can change people's outlook. Even so-called vest-pocket parks or a nearly natural redesign of the residential environment enhance the city as a place to live. This applies especially to areas with high population density and a lack of green open space. But strategies for renaturation must not be limited to individual projects.

If the demolishing of buildings in high-density locations is followed by newly-gained open spaces, the residential environment becomes more attractive. In the best case, even small green spaces and so-called vest-pocket parks can develop the quality of the site in terms of microclimate. Areas to be renaturated at the city's edge open up new opportunities to interlink the city and the landscape. Especially in terms of the urban climate, the principle of demolition 'from the outside in' should be complemented by structuring the urban space with favorably structured networks of green corridors and green axes as well as green 'oases'.

3.4 Renaturation – With Tenacity and a Strategic Concept

Renaturation projects have a long time frame. At first, successes can be made out only in individual places. Renaturation projects grow, change, and become more differentiated. Concepts are to be designed dynamically, which requires open processes and permits making corrections. The openness of many renaturation processes is a great challenge for political and administrative actors, the business world, and the citizenry. Nature teaches us that everything is constantly undergoing transformation. Fixed plans would not do justice to this phenomenon.

Site-specific demolition and returning land are to be developed as forward strategies. The debate about designing material flows in loops, which is quite advanced, has not yet taken the resource land into account sufficiently. However, its quality of being finite is easy to comprehend. The topic of 'renaturation' in connection with urban development has been gaining increasing attention recently (BMVBS/BBSR, 2009c). Nonetheless it requires perseverance in the long term to convey these new challenges to sustainable urban development policy. Returning built-up land means breaking new ground, for no established practice exists. Legal tools and planning procedures are designed to guide orderly urban development. Open spaces have traditionally been understood in planning practice as 'land to be kept free of development'. We still need to learn how to develop formerly built-up areas into new landscapes. The real test for such reclaimed areas is whether or not the public accepts them.

4. Conclusion

'Stadtumbau-Ost' and 'Stadtumbau-West' have much in common, but each program also has its special features. The commonalities include the underlying conditions, which in the final analysis are the expression of global developments. These expressions of demographic and economic trends can also be observed in other European countries. The decline of the population in Germany from 83 million to between 69 and 73 million in 2030 is no longer a phenomenon specific to eastern Germany, but will also have effects in western German regions, especially in old industrialized parts of the country.

The commonalities also include the observation that especially in light of increased globalization, a return to local characteristics is increasing. Even if the term 'Heimat' (homeland) cannot be used with ease, due to Germany's history, urban neighborhoods as everyday living environments are becoming increasingly important – in both eastern and western areas.

An important difference between eastern and western Germany lies not only in the vehemence with which the process of transformation has taken place so far. Just as important are the backdrops to urban development. In western areas, urban restructuring is characterized by an almost 40-year tradition of cautious measures of urban development grants, and it took place in older neighborhoods. In eastern areas, in contrast, it is especially the neighborhoods developed during recent decades, where urban development grants promoted massive demolition, where urban restructuring is taking place, while only in recent years has attention turned to older urban neighborhoods.

Common to the two program areas is the fact that they provide urban development responses to structural social and economic change. Shrinkage and growth are parallel processes – at the national, urban-regional, and urban scales. Renaturation and interim uses are proving to be a dual strategy of sustainable urban development that people are still unaccustomed to, but it will become increasingly important in the future.

References

Baumgartner, D. & Seidl, I. (2008). Rückzonung – eine Herausforderung für die kommunale Nutzungsplanung. *disp, 173, 2*, pp. 22-32.

Becker, C. & Giseke U. (2004). Wildnis als Baustein künftiger Stadtentwicklung. *Garten + Landschaft, 2*, pp. 22-23.

BMVBS (2008). *Evaluierung des Bund-Länder-Programms Stadtumbau Ost*. Berlin.

BMVBS (2007). *5 Jahre Stadtumbau Ost – zweiter Statusbericht*. Berlin.

BMVBS/BBR (2008). Zwischennutzungen und Nischen. *Werkstatt:Praxis, 57*. Bonn.

BMVBS/BBR (2004). *Zwischennutzungen und neue Freiflächen*. Berlin.

BMVBS/BBSR (2009a). *Nutzung städtischer Freiflächen für erneuerbare Energien*. Bonn.

BMVBS/BBSR (2009b). Leitfaden zum Einsatz von Rechtsinstrumenten beim Umgang mit verwahrlosten Immobilien ("Schrottimmobilien"). *Werkstatt:Praxis, 65*. Bonn.

BMVBS/BBSR (2009c). Renaturierung als Strategie nachhaltiger Stadtentwicklung. *Werkstatt:Praxis, 62*. Bonn.

BMVBW (2000). *Bericht der Kommission "Wohnungswirtschaftlicher Strukturwandel"*. Berlin.

Deutscher Städtetag (1971). *Rettet unsere Städte jetzt!* Stuttgart: Kohlhammer Verlag.

Fuhrich, M. (2009). Renaturierung als Vorwärtsstrategie nachhaltiger Stadtentwicklung. *Informationen zur Raumentwicklung, 7*, pp. 503.

Fuhrich, M. (2003). Stadt retour – Dimensionen und Visionen der "schlanken Stadt". *Informationen zur Raumentwicklung, 10/11*, pp. 589.

Fuhrich, M. & Kaltenbrunner, R. (2005). Der Osten jetzt auch im Westen? *Berliner Debatte Initial, 2*, pp. 41-54.

Giseke, U. (2007). Und auf einmal ist Platz. In U. Giseke & E. Spiegel (eds.), *Stadtlichtungen, Irritationen, Perspektiven, Strategie* (Reihe Bauwelt Fundamente 138). Basel: Birkhäuser.

Häußermann, H. & Siebel, W. (1988). Die schrumpfende Stadt und die Stadtsoziologie. In J. Friedrichs (ed.), *Soziologische Stadtforschung* (pp. 78-94). Opladen: Westdeutscher Verlag.

Heiland, S. (2006). Eine Beziehung besonderer Art – Natur in der Stadt. *Politische Ökologie, 99*.

Le Roy, L. G. (1983). *Natur einschalten – Natur ausschalten*. Frankfurt: Klett-Cotta.

Liebmann, H. & Karsten, M. (2009). Stadtumbau Ost und Stadtumbau West: Geschwister mit Eigenarten und Gemeinsamkeiten. *Informationen zur Raumentwicklung, 7*, pp. 33-36.

Schlegelmilch, F. (2009). Zwischennutzen – leichter gesagt als getan. *Informationen zur Raumentwicklung, 7*, pp. 493-502.

Zapf, K. (1969). *Rückständige Viertel*. Frankfurt: Europäische Verlagsanstalt.

Accomodating Creative Knowledge Workers? Empirical Evidence from Metropoles in Central and Eastern Europe

Joachim Burdack, Bastian Lange

1. Challenging the Creative Paradigm in Central and Eastern European Metropoles – An Outline

The emergence of creative and cultural industries has attracted much attention in urban research on cities in Western Europe and North America. By contrast, little knowledge can be found on the status of creative workers in Central and Eastern Europe. The debate in Western Europe considers creativity and knowledge as central factors in enhancing the competitiveness of the urban economic base. Creative and knowledge-based industries are also gaining increasing importance in post-transition cities in Central and Eastern Europe. This paper presents recent empirical survey results from an international research project involving creative workers in Budapest, Leipzig, Poznan, and Riga. What 'soft' and 'hard' factors attract creative knowledge workers to metropolitan areas in Central and Eastern Europe? What conclusions for policy making can be drawn from the results?

2. Definitions and Theoretical Assumptions

In view of the continuing pressure of the structural transition over the past few years, numerous European metropolitan regions have followed the model of creative and knowledge-based urban development. Innovation, high-tech, and, increasingly, creative workers have become ever more integrated into the development strategies of cities since the mid-1990s. Efforts have been undertaken to link economic, spatial, cultural, and research sectors in order to formulate so called 'creative- and knowledge-based cities'. These symbolic ideals and their factual spatial representations form the framework for highly dynamic, trans-nationally operating creative economies (e. g., advertising, marketing, art, design, fashion, etc.). Innovative and creative milieus appear to have an incubator function for creative industries. As such, their existence would be vital for creating regional competitiveness.

B. Müller, *German Annual of Spatial Research and Policy 2010*,
German Annual of Spatial Research and Policy,
DOI 10.1007/978-3-642-12785-4_6, © Springer-Verlag Berlin Heidelberg 2011

2.1 Defining Creative Industries

Creative knowledge is referred to as the basic resource for the future competitiveness of towns and cities in Europe. According to Richard Florida, a regional economist from the United States, the three 'Ts' – tolerance, talent, and technology – largely determine whether cities successfully position themselves (or not). The assertion is that creative workers do not go to where jobs are located, but that jobs go to where innovative and creative people are. In order for these people to develop, they need a tolerant and receptive urban environment. According to Florida, cities and regions in a globally operating economy can only survive if they attract highly qualified and mobile knowledge workers.

In recent years, the terms 'creative industries' and Richard Florida's 'creative class' have become key concepts to describe the growing number of creative workers in various markets. In general, creative industries comprise the employment sector and thus all companies and the self-employed producing, marketing, distributing, and thus trading of cultural goods. In the course of increasing interest in this policy field, creative industries have been analyzed in relation to urban development (Hospers, 2003), to urban competitiveness (Florida, 2005; Youl Lee, Florida, & Acs, 2004), as well as to organizational changes within small and medium-sized enterprises (Grabher, 2004; Scott, 2006) These all take into account the fact that new combinations of innovative 'knowledge' can restructure economies, public administrations, entrepreneurship, and its socialities (Lange, 2007a). Creative industries are considered to express a new type of labor. New inner-organizational dimensions have been addressed as network-based project ecologies with new entrepreneurial and socio-spatial practices (DeFillippi, Grabher, & Jones, 2007; Lange, 2007a, 2008). As a major target group of the so-called creative city, they might be seen as representatives of new modes of labor, with their self-governing practices in the field of creative industries (Lange, Kalandides, Stöber, & Wellmann, 2009). A professional milieu of micro-companies has emerged especially in the field of symbol-producing service providers (particularly web, print, media, and interior design).

2.2 Creativity and its Pitfalls

Parallel to the growing interest in this issue, critics have become skeptical, because the international – mainly anglophone – discussion in the past few years has tended to be dominated by a euphoric notion of the so-called creative city (Landry, 2001). The site-specific context of the application of the concept has been neglected. There appears to be little doubt that creative industries are the solution to major urban problems such as economic stagnation, urban shrinkage, social segregation, technological ageing, global competition, etc. As a term common in current urban debates, 'creativity' has a thoroughly positive ring to it (Althans, Audehm, Binder, Ege, & Färber, 2008; Lange, 2005) It is also configurable and thus possesses strategic potential, which has raised the interest of policy makers and consultancies in Central and Eastern European metropoles (e.g., O´Connor, 2005).

In opposition to this positive view of creative industries is a growing skeptical discourse, arising not only in academia (Anheier, 2008) but also in the field of creative producers, artists, and core creative agents. They criticize the practicability and the suitability of this grand narrative of 'creative industries' for their individual real-world situations, as well as for the advancement of art, culture, and of symbolic values as such. The concept of creativity can by no means be applied to each region in the same way. The process of transferring the mainly anglophone-based concept to Central and Eastern European metropoles is not easily undertaken. What is often left out in the process of transferring such a concept from its original setting to a new systemic context is the heterogeneity of cultural values.

2.3 The Geographies and Localities of the Creative Industries

From a geographic perspective, the site specific qualities of locations and spatial settings are being put to the fore more than ever in this ongoing debate on the relevance of creative industries as a driver of regional development. That is why 'creative and knowledge-based services' have become the focal point of urban strategies and policies – especially since they have come to occupy an increasingly dominant share of the national income. Creative workers – so the expectations – embody the 'new' and a preference for the 'urban'. As an urban avant-garde with specific spatial and consumption needs, they assist in upgrading and revitalizing certain inner city quarters – something that is being increasingly recognized by the real estate industry (Lange, 2007b). After all, creative workers do not gather where the jobs are, but in attractive residential locations and at the centers of cultural life. This turns classic location theories upside down: The established assumption was that qualified workers would go where they could find jobs ('workers follow jobs'). Now it seems that creative workers choose places with favorable living and working environments and locate their business there ('jobs follow workers'). The creative industries therefore initially represent an economy aligned to ideas, idea generation, and innovation rather than one oriented to series and standardized production. This, in association with other organizational notions of creative work, life styles, and consumption habits, leads to new national and urban geographies as well as a reconsideration of the relationship between hard and soft location factors. Cities, according to Florida (2002, p. 224), are now confronted with the task of not only functionally linking the first locality (private area) with the second one (place of work), but increasingly of providing a third type of locality – i.e., meeting places for interaction, communication, and learning (so-called third spaces). Generating a critical size of interesting locations is instrumental to attracting high-income target groups and thus indirectly as being conducive to urban innovation.

3. Central and Eastern European Metropolitan Areas in Transition: Converging and Diverging Developments in Riga, Budapest, Poznan, and Leipzig

The cities analyzed in this paper differ in their position in national urban hierarchies but they are all major cultural centers and have some potential to develop creative industries. Budapest and Riga are unrivalled capital cities and primate cities in their countries, while Poznan and Leipzig are 'only' large regional centers. A common characteristic of the cities analyzed is that their recent development has been strongly influenced by the political and economic transformation process of the early 1990s. While all four cites were integrated into the planning economies of their countries within the framework of Comecon (Council for Mutual Economic Assistance) before 1990, today they are all part of market economies within the political framework of the European Union. These political and economic changes have caused deep ruptures in the cities' development paths and have also often led to important reorientations with regards to their external international linkages. The manufacturing industries that to a larger or smaller degree formed an important economic basis in the cities during the socialist period were often not able to compete under market conditions, and collapsed or were downsized with extensive job losses. Especially in Budapest, Leipzig, and Riga, the old manufacturing industries left a legacy of large inner city industrial brown fields. In Budapest they form an extensive 'rust belt' around the inner city (Kovács, Egedy, Földi, Kerseztely, & Szabo, 2007). There are various examples of vacant industrial premises being transformed into locations for emerging cultural industries. In Riga abandoned port facilities and warehouses in the Andrejsala area have been converted into galleries and a cultural center. In Leipzig a large historic cotton mill (Baumwollspinnerei) now houses galleries and art studios of international reputation.

The political and economic transformation was probably the least abrupt in the case of Budapest, where the changes were to a certain degree anticipated by economic reforms in the 1970s and 1980s. The Hungarian transition is therefore often considered as an example of 'gradualism'. Riga on the other hand, was confronted with the most dramatic changes. Instead of being an important gateway city to the Soviet Union, it is now the somewhat oversized capital city of a small independent state (Latvia). Riga experienced a drastic decrease in its population from 910,000 in 1989 to 732,000 in 2005. Much of the population loss is due to ethnic Russians who left the city after the independence of Latvia in 1991. Still, more than 40 percent of the population of Riga consists of ethnic Russians (Paalzow, Kilis, Dombrovsky, Pauna, & Sauka, 2007). The 2000s have been marked by a continuing expansion of the service sector in Riga. Financial services have grown particularly rapidly. Leipzig was integrated into a reunited Germany, which meant new challenges and opportunities due to increased competition and a larger market. There was considerable growth in the banking sector and also in the media sector (printing, publishing, and film and TV productions), in logistics, and in automobile production. The city managed to maintain the high status of the Leipzig Trade Fair against strong competition (Lange, Burdack, Herfert, Thalman, & Manz, 2007). Persistent high unemployment remains, however. Poznan profits from its strategic location on the axis between Berlin and Warsaw. The city is the major Polish trade fair and exhibition center and also one of the most important centers for higher education in Poland, with a rich cultural milieu (Stryjakiewicz, Kaczmarek, Meczynski, Rarysek, & Stachowiak, 2007). Although all these cities may be considered 'latecomers' with respect to creative and knowledge-intensive industries, creative and knowledge-based industries already occupy a significant share of their urban work forces (Tab. 1).

Metropolitan area	Creative knowledge sector	Creative industries	Knowledge intensive industries
	% of total employment		
Budapest	29	13	16
Leipzig	25	9	16
Poznan	18	7	11
Riga	29	6	23

Tab. 1: Employment in the creative knowledge sector in Eastern European metropolitan areas 2004-2005. Source: Kovács, Murie, Musterd, Gritsai, and Pethe (2007), p. 22.

4. The Location Decisions of Creative and Knowledge Workers: Survey Results

Data on the location-based decisions of creative and knowledge-intensive workers in Budapest, Leipzig, Poznan, and Riga, which is analyzed in this section, is based on surveys conducted as part of the ACRE-project (Accommodating Creative Knowledge – Competitiveness of European Metropolitan Regions within the Enlarged Union), which is financed within the 'European Union's Sixth Framework Programme'. About 200 creative workers were interviewed in each metropolitan area using a standardized questionnaire. The principal objective of the survey was to understand the factors behind the location decisions of creative workers with regard to living and working in a particular city. This research issue is linked to a debate on the rising importance of 'soft factors' (i.e., the atmosphere of an urban area, an attractive urban environment, tolerance for other lifestyles, etc.) in location decisions, since traditional 'hard' location factors are increasingly ubiquitous.

Empirical results revealed that the basic structure of the most important factors that attract creative workers to a particular location seem to be quite similar in the four metropolitan areas, but that there are also some significant differences

(Tab. 2). The factors 'proximity to family' and 'proximity to friends' were among the top five reasons chosen from an extensive list of 26 items in all cities. The employment-related reasons of good chances of finding a job ('employment opportunities') or 'moved here because of my job' are important factors for moving to a city in all of the research areas except Leipzig. The function of Poznan as an important university town that has more than 100,000 students plays a role in explaining location decisions in favor of the city. 'Studied in Poznan' is mentioned as the single most important factor regarding a move to Poznan. As a general tendency it can be said that the most important attraction factors are thus either 'hard', i.e., often job related factors, or are related to personal ties and social networks the respondents have. Leipzig was the only city for which a 'soft' factor is mentioned among the top five ('friendliness of the city').

Rank	Budapest	Leipzig	Poznan	Riga
	in % of respondents			
1.	Family lives here (47)	Job (74)	Studied here (59)	Employment opportunities (49)
2.	Born here (40)	Friends (36)	Employment opportunities (56)	Family lives here (46)
3.	Friends (40)	Family lives here (35)	Family (46)	Studied here (44)
4.	Job (32)	Friendliness of city (35)	Born here (40)	Born here (42)
5.	Employment opportunities/ Studied here (30)	Housing afford-ability (27)	Friends (39)	Job (42)

Tab. 2: Reasons for living in the metropolitan area (up to four reasons chosen from a list of 26) – most important factors (in percent of respondents). Source: Compiled by the authors from ACRE surveys (2007).

The fact that personal ties, social networks, and hard location factors are more important attractors than soft location factors is confirmed when the scores of all the 26 individual items are taken into consideration. An aggregation of the survey items into the three main factors 'personal and social networks', 'hard location factors' and 'soft location factors' done by Martin-Brelot, Grossetti, Eckert, Gritsai, and Kovács (2009) shows that personal and social network factors play the most important role in creative workers deciding to relocate to Budapest, Riga, and Poznan. This contradicts assumptions of a highly mobile creative class that considers soft location factors as increasingly relevant when making decisions concerning their working and living locations. Soft location factors may, however, still play an important role in retaining creative workers in a city once they have settled there, even if they were initially attracted by other factors.

Metropolitan area	Personal ties and networks	'Hard' factors	'Soft' factors
	in %		
Budapest	71	24	5
Leipzig	43	50	8
Poznan	74	23	2
Riga	80	17	4

Tab. 3: The importance of different groups of location factors (aggregation of individual factors; only the first reason mentioned was included). Source: After Martin-Brelot, Grossetti, Eckert, Gritsai, and Kovács (2009).

The survey results also revealed that creative workers in the two primate cities Budapest and Riga are much more critical about quality of life aspects in their cities than those in Poznan and Leipzig. Satisfaction with public services is significantly lower, and worries about urban problems are often much more pronounced in Budapest and Riga. The main urban issues that Budapest respondents worry about are 'homelessness' (91 percent), 'air pollution' (88 percent) and 'traffic' (73 percent). Traffic is also a major concern in Poznan (83 percent) and Riga (82 percent). The availability of affordable housing is by far the greatest anxiety of the respondents in Poznan (85 percent). In Leipzig, on the other hand, affordable housing is not a worrying issue (14 percent), but the availability of jobs (74 percent) is the main concern. The level of anxiety concerning urban issues and problems (mean score) is significantly lower in Leipzig than in the other three metropolitan areas. The average score on 16 possibly worrying urban issues is 32 percent in Leipzig while it is above 50 percent in the other three cities.

In view of the results presented above, it is not surprising that overall satisfaction with the city ('All things considered, how satisfied are with your life in ...?') is higher in the two regional centers than in the two primate cities. On a scale of 1 to 10, where 1 means very satisfied and 10 means very dissatisfied, the average for Leipzig is 2.9 and for Poznan 3.9. Riga scores 4.2 and Budapest only 5.1. Creative workers in Leipzig obviously appreciate the quality of life in their city. In Latvia and Hungary there are but few alternatives for creative workers outside the capital regions, since most of the creative industries are concentrated there.

5. Accommodating Creative Knowledge Workers? Concluding Statements

Survey results indicate that the degree of mobility of the 'creative class' in Central and Eastern European metropolitan areas should not be overestimated. Policies that aim to increase the creative potential in a city should thus not focus primarily on attracting talent from the outside but on retaining and developing the creative human capital that is already there and has ties to the city. A policy emphasis on retaining and developing local talent has to take into consideration the fact that these creative workers often live on rather low incomes and are thus not attracted by gentrified neighborhoods but look for inexpensive places and spaces to work, live, meet, and experiment. A creative scene might develop better in the context of a loose regulatory framework that permits multiple uses of space as opposed to tightly regulated spatial settings. Urban policies should thus aim to preserve such 'free spaces' in the urban fabric for creative use.

References

Althans, B., Audehm, K., Binder, B., Ege, M. & Färber, A. (2008). Kreativität. Eine Rückrufaktion. *Zeitschrift für Kulturwissenschaften, 1*, pp. 7-13.

Anheier, H. K. (2008). *The Cultural Economy*. Los Angeles: Sage.

DeFillippi, R., Grabher, G. & Jones, C. (2007). Introduction to paradoxes of creativity: managerial and organizational challenges in the cultural economy. *Journal of Organizational Behavior, 28(5)*, pp. 511-521.

Florida, R. (2005). *The Flight of the Creative Class*. New York: Routledge.

Florida, R. (2002). *The Rise of the Creative Class: And how it's Transforming Work, Leisure, Community and Everyday Life*. New York: Basic Books.

Grabher, G. (2004). Temporary Architectures of Learning: Knowledge Governance in Project Ecologies. *Organization studies, 25(9)*, pp. 1491-1514.

Hospers, G.-J. (2003). Creative City: Breeding Places in the Knowledge Economy. *Knowledge, Technology, & Policy, 16(3)*, pp. 143-162.

Kovács, Z., Egedy, T., Földi, Z., Kerseztely, K. & Szabo, B. (2007). *Budapest from state socialism to global capitalism. Pathways to creative and knowledge-based regions* (ACRE report 2.4). Amsterdam: University of Amsterdam.

Kovács, Z., Murie, A., Musterd, S., Gritsai, O. & Pethe, H. (2007). Comparing paths of creative knowledge regions (ACRE report 3). Amsterdam: University of Amsterdam .

Landry, C. (2001). *The creative city. A toolkit for urban innovators* (repr. ed.). London: Earthscan.

Lange, B. (2008). Accessing markets in creative industries – professionalization and social-spatial strategies of culturepreneurs in Berlin. *Creative Industries Journal, 1(2)*, pp. 115-135.

Lange, B. (2007a). *Die Räume der Kreativszenen. Culturepreneurs und ihre Orte in Berlin*. Bielefeld: Transcript Verlag.

Lange, B. (2007b). Unternehmen Zwischennutzung: Nährboden für die Kreativwirtschaft. In K. Overmeyer (ed.), *Urban Pioneers in Berlin* (pp. 135-142). Berlin: Birkhäuser.

Lange, B. (2005). Wachstumsmotor Kreative – Eine Kritik an Richard Florida. In P. Oswalt (ed.), *Schrumpfende Städte – Handlungskonzepte* (Vol. 2, pp. 401-405). Ostfildern/Ruit: Hatje Cantz Verlag.

Lange, B., Burdack, J., Herfert, G., Thalmann, R. & Manz, K. (2007). *Creative Leipzig? Pathways to creative and knowledge-based regions* (ACRE report 2.6). Amsterdam: University of Amsterdam .

Lange, B., Kalandides, A., Stöber, B. & Wellmann, I. (eds.). (2009). *Governance der Kreativwirtschaft: Diagnosen und Handlungsoptionen*. Bielefeld: transcript.

Martin-Brelot, H., Grossetti, M., Eckert, D., Gritsai, O. & Kovács, Z. (2009). Not So Mobile 'Creative Class': A European Perspective**.** *GaWC Research Bulletin 306.* Retrieved from: http://www.lboro.ac.uk/gawc/world2008t.html

O'Connor, J. (2005). Creative Exports: Taking "Cultural Industries" to St Petersburg. *International Journal of Cultural Policy, 11(1)*, pp. 45-59.

Paalzow, A., Kilis, R., Dombrovsky, V., Pauna, D. & Sauka, A. (2007). Riga: From Hanseatic city to modern metropolis. *Pathways to creative and knowledge-based regions* (ACRE report 2.9). Amsterdam: University of Amsterdam.

Scott, A. J. (2006). Entrepreneurship, Innovation and Industrial Development: Geography and the Creative Field Revisited. *Small business economics, 26(1),* pp. 1-24.

Stryjakiewicz, T., Kaczmarek, T., Meczynski, M., Rarysek, J. J. & Stachowiak, K. (2007). Poznan faces the future. *Pathways to creative and knowledge-based regions* (ACRE report 2.8). Amsterdam: University of Amsterdam.

Youl Lee, S., Florida, R. & Acs, Z. (2004). Creativity and Entrepreneurship: A Regional Analysis of New Firm Formation. *Regional studies, 38(8),* pp. 879-892.

A Strategy for Dealing with Change: Regional Development in Switzerland in the Context of Social Capital

Stephan Schmidt

1. Introduction

For decades regional development in Switzerland was characterized by preserving a traditional spatial structure dealing with change more as a threat than an opportunity in the sense of modern renewal. By promoting innovation, spatial reorganization, and strong, future-oriented, sustainable regions this unsatisfying situation is approached by the Swiss 'Neue Regionalpolitik' (NRP). For this purpose a knowledge management system understood as a strategy of social learning has been designed to link social capital-based regional development with elements of sustainability.

The aspired strength of Swiss regions in the context of change can be paraphrased by referring to a striving for regional resilience. Early attempts to define resilience focused on a system's ability to absorb change in order to maintain stability. This view restricts the treatment of change to a conservatory level described in the former Swiss case. But understanding change as bifurcation on trajectories of systems concedes its potential to generate manifold types of progress and space for innovation. This is what Folke (2006) intends when he describes his concept of social-ecological resilience. He points out that the concept of resilience integrates the idea of adaptation, learning, and self-organization. This provides the possibility to emphasize the social dimension, i.e., social capital, of change.

The implications of the term social capital vary according to the author and the scope of application. For this article a minimal consensus is found within the work of Coleman (1988) and Putnam (1993). Accordingly, social capital is defined by its function, i.e., it consists of social structures and facilitates certain actions by actors. It denotes the regular association of people with one another with reference to networks and to a combination of norms and values that emerge in informal or formal relationships. However, Bourdieu's idea of distinguishing between the social relationship itself and the amount and quality of those resources is a valuable enhancement (Portes, 1998). Ideas about social capital have already found their way into organizational theory as well as into recent concepts of spatial development, acknowledging that social resources, understood as the basis of regional cohesion, can provide a structure and framework to react positively to change (Tippelt et al., 2009).

This article starts from a sustainability research perspective and seeks to conceptualize a strategy of regional development that is appropriate to deal with

B. Müller, *German Annual of Spatial Research and Policy 2010*,
German Annual of Spatial Research and Policy,
DOI 10.1007/978-3-642-12785-4_7, © Springer-Verlag Berlin Heidelberg 2011

change in the sense of safeguarding societal functioning, i.e., the ability to act. It states that principal elements of sustainability can likewise function as a basis for a regional development focused on social capital. Accordingly, I draw on the idea of 'learning regions', which ensures the appreciation of social matters for regional development, but has weaknesses in formulating its theoretical basis and in addressing its implementation. In order to fill these gaps, the aforementioned concept of sustainability, with a particular interest in a set of instrumental rules, is considered to be a basic prerequisite. For the purpose of implementation an approach of social learning is introduced as a tool and integrated into the development strategy through the theories of actor-networks and communities of practice.

The presented theoretical elements of such a development strategy for dealing with change can be associated with the Swiss NRP. The idea behind the NRP seems to consider both the meaning of social capital as well as a broad understanding of learning for development. One of the basic features of the NRP is the implementation of the aforementioned knowledge management to support crucial actors and to give them opportunities to create individual strategies for change. Underlying is the implicit assumption that this type of management will lead to and spread sustainable solutions within Swiss regions. An empirical survey of the Swiss case will scrutinize both: First, the potential of the NRP to satisfy the requirements of the presented strategy to deal with change, and second, the contribution of the NRP to sustainable regional development in Switzerland.

2.   The Implementation of Sustainability

Since this article does not allow for outlining a comprehensive concept of sustainability, it focuses on the implementation of sustainability understood as a concept that aims at safeguarding the ability to undertake societal action.

More or less in parallel to the general discussion about sustainability as the leading model for shaping our future, research on social matters identified social capital as being a crucial factor in the achievement of sustainable development (Grunwald & Kopfmueller, 2006). The aim of this kind of development is to find explanations and solutions for developmental problems (foundation) and the implementation of the same (practice). Emphasizing the role of social capital in this context means to understand sustainability as a future-oriented societal process of learning and searching. This means we need to develop appropriate knowledge, skills, values, and attitudes. Thus, learning for sustainability is a lifelong process that is influenced by the social and environmental contexts in which it takes place (Birney, Hren, Jackson, & Kendell, 2006). The main question with regard to the implementation of this process points to the 'how'. How can the learning process for sustainability be implemented? A guideline for this purpose has to encompass a set of instrumental rules. The following sections will elucidate on this: What are the central aspects of this set of rules? Where did the rules originated? And most important of all, which purpose shall they serve?

Concerning the last question, the clarification of the purpose or task of the instrumental rules is of central importance. Talking about a concept of sustainability in this relationship requires the aforementioned distinction between a foundational and a practical layer. The latter deals with the established three or four dimensions derived from the typical 'Tripple Bottom Line'. With regard to this article, the practical layer shapes a possible solution for a problem of regional development policy and finally facilitates its implementation. The explanation for and the response to this problem is given by a foundational layer and its elements, considering on the one hand the issue of (intra- and intergenerational) justice and on the other hand the issue of dependency of society and nature, with both issues being correlated by a theory of goods. The purpose of the instrumental rules is now to facilitate the transformation from the foundational to the practical layer as described above.

To understand the prerequisites of these instrumental rules, one has to have recourse to the aforementioned theory of goods and to capabilities in the sense of Nussbaum and Sen (1993). To cut right to the chase, capabilities are the internal and non-material resources required by humans to transform their disposition to act, respectively their intention, into concrete actions. But action does not exclusively depend on internal resources, but also on external conditions with individual and societal relatedness. Kopfmueller et al. (2001) capture this point by formulating a set of substantial 'what' rules – minimal requirements of sustainability on an individual basis – and instrumental 'how' rules, whereas the latter tend to describe the required societal functions for living an action-guided life. Criticism of the alignment, as well as of the conceptualizing of these 'how' rules in respect of the transformation purpose reflects the starting point of a rethinking of the 'instrumental rules'.

In fact, this paper identifies four central issues that should be maintained and fostered in the proposed concept. Sustainable economic or social activities are often linked to a demand for increased innovation ability. Innovation means to create, to undertake, and to successfully use improvements in the economy and society. In addition, the process of sustainable development demands a reliable knowledge basis, in particular to specify the concept of sustainability, for the diagnosis of sustainability problems, and for the development of applicable therapies (Dybowski & Haertel, 2003). Thus, knowledge transfer does not only mean sending or delivering knowledge from one place or person to another, it also concerns the identification, communication, and sharing of knowledge. Furthermore, strategies for sustainable development have to be based on inherent criteria, what means that community members have to have the ability to adjust to a societal disequilibrium within mutual learning processes. The basis for this self-organization is constituted by both the mode of monitoring – the interaction between the individual and his or her environment – and reflexivity, which is understood as the perception and enunciation of problems and the ability of knowing action under varying conditions. The fourth and last issue is the ability to plan and implement strategies for sustainable development, which is widely paraphrased as capacity-building. It is primarily intended to enhance people's capacity to be aware of and to articulate their own interests as well as to determine their own values and priorities in the context of sustainable development rather than strengthening institutions in general. This set of instrumental rules – innovation ability, knowledge transfer, self-organization, and capacity-building – builds a foundation for the strategy to implement sustainability. The application of such a strategy in the context of regional development could be facilitated through a social learning approach.

3. Social Learning as a Tool

Theories about social learning can be traced back to criticism of conventional conceptions of human learning as an individual phenomenon. In contrast to this idea, learning is seen as being embedded in social practices, activities, and interactions. Thus, learning is something that occurs between people and within groups of persons and tends to support concerted action in the light of complexity and uncertainty. Learning is about developing adaptive cross-sectoral and new relational capacities as well as new types of knowledge (Pahl-Wostl, Mostert, & Tàbara, 2008). Social learning in this context could support the implementation of the instrumental rules of sustainability in a context of regional development, and is thus suitable for an integrated application.

Processes of social learning take place in networks and communities of practice (Pahl-Wostl, Mostert, & Tàbara, 2008), and benefit therefore from social and spatial proximity. Networking has been shown to be a crucial element of regional development, because it provides stakeholders with access to resources and knowledge. The purpose of an application of a network-theory is hereby the understanding of organizational changes through the attitudes, constructions, and cognitions of the acting stakeholders (so-called actors). According to Mueller-Prothmann (2006), a network is defined by its nodes and relationships, and one could say that it is a set of actors and the relationships between them. Within this approach, attention is paid particularly to the central nodes of the network or obligatory points of passage, facilitating the translation of an individual problem into a common one (Fox, 2000). Actors enrolled in a network move through this passage point and thus contribute to the routinization and durability of the network. In this sense, Communities of Practice (CoP) could serve as obligatory passage points, because a CoP is a node for the exchange and interpretation of information, as well as a place for the development of a common comprehension of a theme or problem. CoPs are "groups of people informally bound together by shared expertise and passion for a joint enterprise [...] people in communities of practice share their experiences and knowledge in free-flowing, creative ways that foster new approaches to problems" (Wenger & Snyder, 2000, pp. 139). The concept of CoPs in general is instrumentalized for the direct generation and sharing of knowledge in a context of knowledge management.

In conclusion, social learning through the advancement of CoPs in conjunction with a theory of networks can facilitate a basic learning process for the implementation of the instrumental rules of sustainability. Applied in the context of social capital-based regional development, the social learning tool has the potential to provide an environment for a successful strategy for dealing with change. The idea of a 'learning region' promises to be the spatial concept that has the ability to consider the requirements of this strategy.

4.   Learning Regions as a Path for Dealing with Change

This section will attempt to identify a spatial development strategy that allows for a linkage between social matters of regional development and the instrumental rules of sustainability. Hence, attention is turned to the concept of 'learning regions', accepting that it has weaknesses in its foundation and implementation. Generally, one can describe a region as a contiguous territorial system of interaction and define it through its density of interaction networks. A 'learning region' in turn, encompasses the local and regional socio-cultural dimension, the institutional setting, and social networking as basic prerequisites and focuses on the processes of learning and innovating (Butzin, 2000). The 'learning regions' serve as "repositories of knowledge and ideas, and provide an underlying environment or infrastructure which facilitates the flow of knowledge, ideas and learning" (Florida, 1995, p. 528). Obviously, the idea of learning is inhered by both the social capital-based concept of 'learning regions' and the understanding of sustainability as a societal learning process. This opens up an opportunity to merge the elements of the two approaches and gives the concept of a 'learning region' a stable basis.

Knowledge transfer as one of the instrumental rules also has a high significance for a 'learning region' due to its nature of geographic, cultural, and social proximity. This proximity and its related interpersonal, face-to-face contacts and personal relationships are the basis for the production and the flow of tacit knowledge, which is embedded in the know-how and practices of regional stakeholders. Knowledge in this sense is idiosyncratic and context-specific, but the exchange as well as the production depends on social processes (Uyarra, 2005). Moreover, knowledge represents the basis for regional innovation ability and processes – the second instrumental rule – and for that reason acts as an impetus for the region's renewal, re-organization, and development. But as Tippelt et al. (2009) point out, the concept of 'learning regions' tends to promote the idea that the potential of the regional stakeholder on the whole is activated and used. Accordingly, social capital-based regional development is seen as a self-organized and self-responsible process. This third instrumental rule – self-organization – serves as the basis for the ability to act with a link to regional development as well as in the context of sustainability. The fourth issue, i.e., capacity building, is about improving networking and stakeholder dialogue in a region, about forming partnerships and alliances, and about enhancing the ability to evaluate and address questions related to a region's development.

A 'learning region' focuses on the integration of regional subsystems, institutions, and stakeholders in a process of mutual learning, whereas certain foundational elements of sustainability, i.e., instrumental rules, give the concept a stable theoretical basis. This is facilitated and implemented through an approach of social learning and, finally reflects a self-contained strategy of dealing with change. The Swiss NRP and its knowledge management implicitly refer to this idea of a 'learning region' and thus provide the principles for a successful strategy for dealing with change.

5.   An Empirical Survey of the Swiss Case

The empirical survey is based on the Swiss case, i.e., the Swiss NRP. This federal initiative, amongst other things, aims at the implementation of a formal knowledge management system supporting its participants on an individual and organizational level, and the regional development in Switzerland in general. The initiative intends to lead to and spread sustainable solutions on a regional pattern in Switzerland, whereas system-relevant stakeholders of Swiss regional policy improve their ability to react positively to change.

The project presented conducts the scientific accompanying research of the knowledge management (KM) and has been ongoing for two years. The purpose of the survey is to estimate the contribution of knowledge management to sustainable regional development in Switzerland, and to judge whether the Swiss strategy satisfies the requirements of a strategy for dealing with change or not. The investigation represents a three-stage approach: participant tracking in order to evaluate the scope of the KM, i.e., the CoPs, an ethnographical observation to systemize its functionality, and an interview block to validate insights.

In a first step, federal efforts to implement an institutional KM have to be judged and legitimized. Thus, an evaluation of the scope and range of the KM had to be made. For this reason, tracking participants of the KM has allowed for the creation of individual profiles and shed light on the institutional background of stakeholders. Hence, it is recognizable that participants with a cantonal, regional, non-organizational, or academic background are likewise involved, and nearly to the same (high) extent. It follows that the KM activates stakeholders at all system-relevant layers. The motivation of the participants is mostly generated by the wish to get or stay connected with colleagues, to facilitate an informal exchange (both soft factors), and by the wish to become informed and updated with current information about task-relevant issues (hard factor). The KM responds to the demands of participants with a hybrid strategy. It promotes a personification strategy to guarantee the face-to-face contact, as well as a codification strategy for stimulating the flow of knowledge. But it turns out that the motivation of participants was in flux. At the beginning it was more important to get basic information, e.g., about the new NRP program, because new persons had to accomplish new tasks. Later, due to the maturity of relationships between participants, the soft facts got the centre stage. Thus, the idea behind the KM to promote CoPs as new nodes of a network of regional policy and to bring individual stakeholders together within these CoPs was successful. The results of the CoP's activity were spread throughout the entire system of regional policy by a formally institutionalized means of transfer (web portal, or newsletter) as well as through informal connections between participants within the network, whereas the functioning and significance of the latter have to be further investigated. An initial conclusion is that KM within the NRP became an established and acknowledged institution within the system of regional policy in Switzerland and has had a large-scaled and structuralized impact on the community.

The empirical survey's second step is grounded in an ethnographic observation and comprises a systematizing of the functionality of CoPs, leading to a basic clarification of the impact of KM. This allows insight to be gained into the processes and routines of the CoPs in order to evaluate the contribution KM has made to sustainable regional development. For this purpose it is necessary to monitor the implementation of the instrumental rules of sustainability in the context of regional development. It has yet to be stated that the KM takes action in the fields of knowledge-transfer and the ability for self-organization among stakeholders. First and foremost the elementary processes of knowledge-transfer, the transformation from tacit to explicit knowledge, are facilitated by the work of the CoPs. Indeed, a vital knowledge-transfer is one of the core characteristics of a KM. It turns out, however, that a large majority of participants is willing to contribute their own (tacit) knowledge to the CoP. The community collects this knowledge, generates new knowledge, and finally explicates this knowledge for the benefit of all stakeholders. It is additionally recognizable that the addressing of an individual problem of one participant or a group of participants within a CoP entails a common response and explanation about this issue. In the end this strengthens the role of the CoP as an obligatory point of passage and thus, as a node of the network. If knowledge is a prerequisite for the implementation of sustainability, the Swiss community succeeds at this point. In addition, the CoPs present a widely observable informational openness and recursive interaction. Participants have reported attempts to apply their newly acquired abilities, whether successful or not. This means that the community tends to organize itself.

A different situation arises regarding both the ability to innovate and capacity-building. The monitoring of CoPs has not yet provided any insights into either of these criteria. Regarding the ability to innovate, this may refer to an assumption that KM only attracts stakeholders who are already equipped with this ability. All others may generally stay away from KM. Beyond that, capacity-building among stakeholders probably has the status of an outcome. It is very possible that the ability to determine one's own values and priorities and to know how to help oneself takes time, that the strengthening of vertical and horizontal relationships requires patience, and in general, that capacity-building occurs outside CoPs. But validating these insights and the former one as well requires a third step. This step comprises face-to-face interviews and promises clarification at all levels. This will be done in the next stage of the project.

6. Conclusion

Searching for a comprehensive strategy for dealing with change in the context of regional development means taking advantage of the incorporation of different approaches. One possible path is the interpretation of the idea of 'learning regions' on the basis of the instrumental rules of sustainability implemented through an approach of social learning as a tool. This people-centered approach focuses on the social capital of regions and their stakeholders, provides a necessary future-orientation, and thus sets the stage for inherent, sustainable development as a response or positive reaction to change. The Swiss knowledge management survey provides the first insights into its scope and functionality, and therefore contributes to the clarification of two issues. First, the conceptualization of a strategy to deal with change as it is described in Sections 2 and 4 can be applied to the 'Swiss Case' to a large extent. Both the instrumental principles of sustainability as well as the mechanisms of a social learning approach can be addressed by knowledge management. But it is still not resolved if the spatial substantiation through the implicit underlying idea of 'learning regions' facilitates the implementation of a strategy for dealing with change. This issue needs further clarification. Second, the impact of knowledge management on sustainable regional development in Switzerland is partly positive. While it strengthens at least two instrumental principles, namely the transfer of knowledge and self-organization, participants of knowledge management, and in the end the entire system of regional policy, benefit from the improved ability to act, which is the prerequisite for societal development.

References

Birney, A., Hren, B., Jackson, L. & Kendell, P. (2006). Creating Pathways to Change. In W. Leal Filho (ed.), *Innovation, Education and Communication for Sustainable Development* (pp. 67-84). Frankfurt/M.: Peter Lang.

Butzin, B. (2000). Netzwerke, Kreative Milieus und Lernende Regionen: Perspektiven für die regionale Enzwicklungsplanung? *Zeitschrift für Wirtschaftsgeographie, 3/4*, pp 149-166.

Coleman, J. (1988). Social Capital in the Creation of Human Capital. *The American Journal of Sociology, 94*, pp. 95-120.

Dybowski, G. & Haertel, M. (2003). Trends in der Wissensgesellschaft – Zugang zu Information, Wissen und Bildung. In J. Kopfmueller (ed.), *Den globalen Wandel gestalten. Forschung und Politik für einen nachhaltigen globalen Wandel* (pp. 75-91). Berlin: sigma edition.

Florida, R. (1995). Toward the Learning Region. *Futures, 27/5*, pp. 527-536.

Folke, C. (2006). Resilience: The emergence of a perspective for social-ecological systems analyses. *Global Environmental Change, 16*, pp. 253-267.

Fox, S. (2000). Communities of Practice, Focault and Actor-Network Theory. *Journal of Management Studies, 37:6*, pp. 853-867.

Grunwald, A. & Kopfmueller, J. (2006). *Nachhaltigkeit.* Frankfurt/M.: Campus Verlag.

Kopfmueller, J., Brandl, V., Jörissen, J., Paetau, M., Brause, G., Coenen, R. & Grunwald, A. (2001). *Nachhaltige Entwicklung integrativ betrachtet. Konstitutive Elemente, Regeln, Indikatoren.* Berlin: sigma edition.

Mueller-Prothmann, T. (2006). *Leveraging Knowledge Communication for Innovation. Framework, Methods and Applications of Social Network Analysis in Research and Development.* Frankfurt/M.: Peter Lang.

Nussbaum, M. & Sen, A. (eds.) (1993). *The Quality of Life.* Oxford: Clarendon Press.

Pahl-Wostl, C., Mostert, E. & Tàbara, D. (2008). The Growing Importance of Social Learning in Water Resource Management and Sustainability Science. *Ecology and Society, 13/1*, p. 24.

Portes, A. (1998). Social Capital: Its Origins and Applications in Modern Sociology. *Annual Review of Sociology, 24*, pp. 1-24.

Putnam, R. (1993). The Prosperous Community: Social Capital and Public Life. *The American Prospect, 13*.

Tippelt, R., Reupold, A., Strobel, C., Kuwan, H., Pekince, N., Fuchs, S., Abicht, L. & Schönfeld, P. (eds.) (2009). *Lernende Regionen – Netzwerke gestalten. Teilergebnisse zur Evaluation des Programms "Lernende Regionen – Förderung von Netzwerken".* Bielefeld: Bertelsmann Verlag.

Uyarra, E. (2005). Knowledge, Diversity and Regional Innovation Policies: Theoretical Issues and Empirical Evidence of Regional Innovation Strategies. *PREST Discussion Paper Series*, pp. 5-16.

Wenger, E. & Snyder, W. (2000). Communities of Practice: The Organizational Frontier. *Harvard Business Review, 78:1,* pp. 139-145.

Path Dependency and Resilience – The Example of Landscape Regions

Andreas Röhring, Ludger Gailing

1. Problem Statement

Spatial development is caught somewhere between stability and adaptation to new challenges. The reasons for this are natural risks, as well as dynamic processes of economic and social change, and globalization. In view of increasing risks (cf. Beck, 2007), the resilience of cities and regions is becoming more and more of an issue. The resilience concept, which was originally developed to explain ecological processes, has been further developed and applied to social problems. This has led to links with the social science approach of path theory. In the following article the inhibiting and promoting effects path dependency has on resilience in spatial and social science contexts will therefore be explored and empirically supported.

First of all the theoretical approach to path dependency needs to be introduced, the connection to the resilience concept investigated, and the value of both for an analysis of the stability and adaptability of regions facing new challenges elaborated upon (Section 2). Questions about resilience will not only be dealt with in the context of natural risks, but also with regard to the problems of regional development, using the example of the path dependency of selected landscape regions (Section 3). As socio-spatial constructs, landscape regions are characterized by their cultural identity, common history, and typical forms of land use and settlement structures, which have identity and image-forming effects. Closely related to this, landscape regions can also develop into action arenas due to new forms of governance (cf. Fürst, Gailing, Pollermann, & Röhring, 2008). The article concludes with a comparative interpretation of the empirical results and with inferences for the linking of resilience concepts and path-dependency approaches in socio-scientific spatial research (Section 4).

2. The Benefit of Linking Path Dependency and Resilience

2.1 The Epistemic Value of Theoretical Approaches to Path Dependency

The main thesis of this approach, which was originally used for economic research, is that path dependencies arise when, during the spontaneous processes of development that occur as a result of prior decisions, the path chosen is stabilized

B. Müller, *German Annual of Spatial Research and Policy 2010*,
German Annual of Spatial Research and Policy,
DOI 10.1007/978-3-642-12785-4_8, © Springer-Verlag Berlin Heidelberg 2011

through positive feedback. Because of the resulting dependencies, considerable effort is required to depart from this development path. This is the distinction between 'path-dependent' development processes and those generally influenced by history ('past-dependent') (cf. Araujo & Harrison, n.d.). This theoretical approach explains why, in contrast to the views of neoclassical economists (according to which the markets are dominated by the most efficient technologies), sub-optimal solutions are able to emerge and establish themselves permanently.

The initial phase of a development path (the 'critical juncture') is started by a sequence of random and insignificant events and leads to a first determination of the direction things will move in. As the process continues, the scope of searching for alternatives is increasingly restricted because of specific investments and increasing returns. In this way path dependency becomes more firmly established, and the search for a direction is terminated ('lock-in'). Even if inefficiencies emerge along the trajectory, and 'decreasing returns' begin to occur, the development path may remain quite stable for an extended period of time. This will remain the case until path development stops, either as a result of a modification caused by evolutionary changes or because of external or internal influences (cf. Theuvsen, 2004).

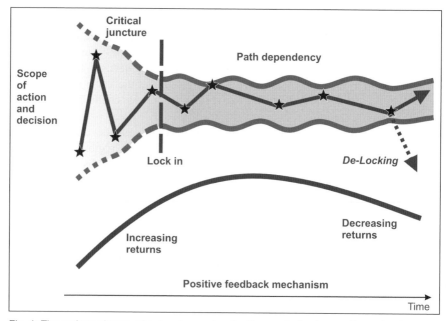

Fig. 1: The various phases of a development path. Source: Author's own illustration (adapted from Schreyögg, Sydow, and Koch, 2003, p. 286).

An extension of the path concept to institutional research (e.g., David, 1994; North 1990), organizational theory (e.g. Schreyögg, Sydow, & Koch, 2003), political science (e.g. Mayntz, 2002; Pierson, 2000), and agricultural economy (e.g. Theuvsen, 2004) has led to a greater appreciation of the influence actors' behavior and institutions – from a social science perspective these are understood as rules – can have. Because of institutional density a great variety of institutions interact with one another (cf. Young, 2002). On the one hand this creates path-stabilizing complementarity effects between institutions (Pierson, 2000). On the other hand, however, due to their inertia, institutions which have been successfully used in previous problematic situations can also create restrictions with regard to solving new problems (Mayntz, 2002). And thus, specific patterns of organizational behavior (Schreyögg et al., 2003), sectoral logics of action, a hardening of mental models, and efforts to maintain power (Pierson, 2000) can all lead to path dependencies.

As a result the theoretical approach to path dependency was not only applied to spontaneous development processes, but also to processes that are consciously influenced (cf. Theuvsen, 2004). This is particularly the case regarding the question of what possibilities actors have to terminate inefficient paths, or rather to initiate a new development path. To this end, Garud and Karnøe (2001) extended the concept of path dependency by using the approach of path creation through mindful deviation from existing development paths. Path creation, however, does not mean that actors can make strategic decisions independent of recent developments. It does, however, offer the potential of a conscious application of path dependency mechanisms within the framework of the management of regional development processes. These extensions of the theoretical approach also allow for new applications concerning the problems of spatial development (cf. Fürst et al., 2008).

2.2 Investigating the Relationship between Path Dependency and Resilience

The resilience concept, which was originally developed by Holling (1973) as an approach to ecological research, aims at the dynamic development of ecosystems and the maintenance of their functions. It is thus in contrast to a rigid and inflexible understanding of stability and balance with regards to internal and external influences. According to Walker, Holling, Carpenter, and Kinzig (2004), resilience is "the capacity of a system to absorb disturbance and reorganize while undergoing change so as to still retain essentially the same function, structure, identity, and feedbacks". Holling and Gunderson (2002) understand resilience as a characteristic of a dynamic model of adaptive cycles in which a system that is caught between conservation and innovation reorganizes itself. The approach has since been extended to social-ecological systems (Walker et al., 2002) in which actors are an integral part of the system and either actively influence its resilience (adaptability) or create a new system (transformability).

It remains unclear, however, just what the mechanisms of self-stabilization are, which driving forces influence the adaptive cycle, and what flexibility and limits actors have regarding the adaptation and transformation of development processes. This is where links to institutionally-based theoretical path approaches play a role. We therefore propose looking at increasing und decreasing returns as an explanation for the stabilization and destabilization, or rather the transformation of development processes. As resilience only describes the ability to adapt to new conditions, however, an understanding of the specific goals of public welfare (cf. Bernhardt, Kilper, & Moss, 2009) is always necessary. This would allow for the resilience concept to be used as a way of ensuring the adaptability and flexibility of path path development and path creation. Tab. 1 gives an overview of both approaches.

Dimension	Theoretical approach of path dependency	Resilience concept
Disciplinary affiliations	Economy	Ecology
Original objective	Establishment of technological development	Adaptability of ecosystems
Extension of the approach	Socio-scientific problems connected with the development of organizations and institutions	Problems connected with the development of social-ecological systems and their vulnerability to natural catastrophes
Explanatory value	Formation of development paths and the dependence mechanisms of their stabilization	Maintenance or restoration of a system's functions and its adaptability
Main categories	Critical junctures, look-in, increasing and/or decrasing returns, mindful deviation	Maintenance or restoration of a system's functions and its adaptability

Tab. 1: A comparison of path dependency and resilience. Source: Compiled by the authors (2010).

3.   Landscape Regions as an Example

In the following section path dependency and resilience will be applied to spatial science problems using the example of landscape regions. Social and ecological problems are closely intertwined in landscape regions due to their multifunctionality. The development of these regions is affected by natural hazards as well as by gradual change. A special feature of landscape regions is that they are common goods and are largely a by-product of the impact of institutions and market incentives. Their development is also strongly influenced by informal institutions (cf. Röhring & Gailing, 2005). This leads to consequences for management approaches, which focus on a strengthening of resilience and thereby have to be able to deal with the impact of path dependencies.

- The example of the Oderbruch illustrates which potentials and problems are connected to the creation of resilience in a landscape region characterized by strong physical, infrastructural, and institutional path dependencies (see 3.1).
- The example of the Barnim examines how corrections to an existing path are being attempted, with the goal of a deliberate departure from influential spatial developments (see 3.2).

3.1 The Effects of Physical and Institutional Path Dependencies on the Resilience of the Oderbruch as a Polder Landscape

The Oderbruch is a region on the German-Polish border that was originally a natural river polder and wetlands landscape dominated by fishing and grassland farming. From an ecological perspective, it once had a resilient ecosystem. A new regional development path was created in 1747 by the implementation of a master plan initiated by Prussian King Friedrich II. This plan included the construction of a new channelized riverbed for the Oder River, drainage measures, and the development of settlement structures in the polder. The necessary reduction of vulnerability to floods and the protection of agricultural production led to new demands on the resilience of the Oderbruch that were shaped by social goals. Measures undertaken to drain the region, which were originally oriented toward improving public welfare, are now (from an environmental perspective) considered to have been a "conquest of nature" (Blackbourn, 2006).

The capital expenditures necessary for the drainage measures led to a lock-in, making it difficult to abandon the chosen development path. The Oderbruch continued to be affected by flooding even after drainage measures were carried out, however. And thus for 250 years development was characterized by the same general principles and logic of action that aimed at perfecting flood management and drainage in order to further intensify land use. This occurred in line with the technological advances made in water management (cf. Quast & Ehlert, 2005).

This logic of action reached its peak in the 1960s as a result of East German agricultural land improvement measures that were based on central policy decisions. The goal of industrial-scale production through the use of machinery on large fields led to an extreme intensification of drainage measures. Increasing economic costs resulted in decreasing returns, which pointed to the limitations of this kind of logic. It also negatively affected the ecological and agricultural potential of this distinctive landscape region.

The general public became aware of the Oderbruch during the severe flooding of 1997, when the complete inundation of this landscape region was only narrowly avoided. In terms of resilience, the floods led to ambivalent reactions. The insurance industry raised the question of whether any further settlement in the area made sense at all. This would have been a deliberate break from a 250-year-old development path because of a completely different social construction of resilience. The state government in Brandenburg made it clear that it was in favor of maintaining the Oderbruch as a settled polder region and took measures to improve flood management.

Given the strong existing path dependencies, the question arises of what restrictions and scope of action for adaptation strategies should be considered with regards to the future development of the Oderbruch. The resilience of this landscape region cannot only be judged according to its vulnerability to flooding, but must also consider the problems of demographic and economic change. Institutional processes of change, such as the 'Water Framework Directive' and 'Natura 2000', are also relevant. And therefore, an interpretation of resilience that considers the multifunctional nature of landscape regions should not only focus on the risk of floods, but also on socially constructed aspects of a sustainable water and land use regime, and the development of the potential offered by a historic cultural landscape in order to do justice to the dialectic of physical-material and social phenomena.

3.2 The Social Construction of Resilience Using the Example of Attempts to Correct the Development Path in the Barnim Region

Research into suburbanization has noted the increasing autonomy of suburban areas (cf. Burdack & Hesse, 2006). In the Barnim, a landscape region to the northeast of Berlin, a functional enhancement of suburbia can also be observed with regards to housing, retail, and trade. This can be interpreted as a suburban development path supported by stabilizing factors that are linked to increasing returns:

- Formal institutions (e.g., a commuting allowance, land-use plans) that influence decisions to locate to a particular area,
- Local community growth objectives determined by the financial interests of attracting new residents and businesses,
- Growth-based coalitions, primarily supported by politicians and businesses, that profit from an expansion of residential and commercial areas,
- Infrastructural investment in the development of residential and commercial areas.

Among the attempts to correct this dominant development path and to initiate alternative, landscape-based regionalization processes in some areas of the Barnim, the 'Naturpark Barnim' and the 'Regionalpark Barnimer Feldmark' have been the most successful. Both are rooted in planning ideas that seek to protect the Barnim landscape region from Berlin's expanding suburbanization and maintain it as an attractive recreational area.

The formulation of the idea of a Naturpark Barnim (nature park) by local conservationists can be interpreted as the critical juncture of an attempted path correction. This constituted positive feedback and steps were taken to establish the Naturpark as a large protected area, i.e., anchoring the idea in local politics, a formal declaration of the area as a nature park, and the creation of a park administration. The Naturpark Barnim can be considered the positive product of an intentional correction of the dominant development path.

Unlike the Naturpark Barnim, the Regionalpark Barnimer Feldmark is not a formal reserve, but an informal instrument used to enhance an agricultural area within the Barnim region. A different institutional context thus provides the possibilities of correcting the suburban development path here: informal actor-based factors are of great relevance instead of formal components. The founding of a regional park association in 1996 is considered the critical juncture in this case. The idea of developing regional parks in the areas surrounding Berlin was first formulated by the joint state planning department of Berlin and Brandenburg (cf. Kühn & Gailing, 2008). By obtaining project funding, association members secure the regional park's capacity to operate. Positive feedback concerning the stabilization of path correction is dependent on these members' active participation. Networking with other associations and community organizations is also of great importance, as is the participation of local farmers and tourist organizations.

In creating both of these path corrections, recreation, nature conservation, and ecological land use as future tasks were discovered after an exploratory phase (cf. Garud & Karnøe, 2001) in order to increase the resilience of the Barnim landscape region with regards to its multifunctionality. The corrections were stabilized in different ways through positive feedback mechanisms (e.g., set-up costs, the effects of learning and coordination, power and legitimacy; cf. Deeg, 2001). While consolidation from the 'top-down' occurred in the Naturpark, and factors such as power and legitimacy played an important roll, in the Regionalpark stabilization was 'bottom-up' due to support by local actors.

Using the example of the Barnim it is possible to show that, on the one hand, the resilience of a landscape region cannot be determined independent of general groups of actors and, on the other hand, it should be linked to the multifunctionality of the landscape. In the end, normative goals are associated with the term 'resilience' that are the subject of processes of social construction (e.g., through regional discourses or regional forms of governance). In the Barnim region there are at least two competing perceptions of resilience: one that supports suburban growth, profits from it, and therefore continues to stabilize it, and one of actors involved in nature park and regional park development who want to preserve the qualitative and ecological aspects of the landscape region as common goods and therefore initiate path corrections. Both groups of actors refer to the same physical and material space, but emphasize different stabilizing elements of the development path they have chosen to pursue.

4. A Comparative Interpretation and Conclusion

The Oderbruch case study shines a light on the difficulties of deviating from a development path chosen in the past, even though excess drainage has led to ecological problems as well as to social problems due to the danger of continued flooding. Such difficulties exist not only with regard to a hardly practicable abandonment of the existing development path, but also with regard to the implementation of path corrections through mindful deviation and to the creation of a multifunctional polder landscape that has a variety of land use restrictions. This clearly illustrates that resilience cannot be reduced to ecological dimensions alone, but must also take their social construction into consideration. An equally dominant development path is found in the Barnim region as well. And, although in contrast to the Oderbruch it even provides substantial 'increasing returns', correction of this path has been possible.

This article has made it obvious that a linkage of the resilience concept with the institutional approach of path dependency promises to be a benefit in terms of explaining spatial development problems from a social science perspective:

- Development paths can lead to both positive and negative effects. For this reason the path concept is analytically suitable for assessing resilience and the adaptability of regional development to new challenges in the form of natural risks and longer-term processes of change. This pertains to the clarification of the role of supportive and restrictive physical-spatial and institutional factors as well as the scope of action of regional actors.

- Securing resilience with the goal of sustainable development may also require the overcoming of an institutional path-dependent logic of action as well as the adaptation of development paths through mindful deviation if they not only lead to stability, but also to inflexibility. To this end regional management approaches and the development of public welfare goals are necessary, so that justice is done to the multifunctionality of spaces, as the example of the Oderbruch landscape region has shown.

At the regional level, however, competing ideas of resilience may emerge due to different interests. This shows that resilience does not manifest itself on the basis of per se ecological criteria, but is rather socially constructed in a dialectic of physical-material and social phenomena. The resilience of a space can be assessed by actors in different ways despite the fact that they have a common spatial reference. Attempts to correct an existing path can be successful if the processes of path creation are supported by increasing returns, as illustrated by the examples of nature park and regional park development in Barnim.

References

Araujo, L. & Harrison, D. (n.d.). *Technological Trajectories and Path Dependence*. Retrieved from: www.bath.ac.uk/imp/pdf/18_AraujoHarrison.pdf

Arthur, W. B. (1994). *Increasing Returns and Path Dependence in the Economy*. Ann Arbor: University of Michigan Press.

Bernhardt, C., Kilper, H. & Moss, T. (eds.) (2009). *Im Interesse des Gemeinwohls. Regionale Gemeinschaftsgüter in Geschichte, Politik und Planung*. Frankfurt/M./ New York: Campus.

Blackbourn, D. (2006). *The Conquest of Nature. Water, Landscape and the Making of Modern Germany*. London: W.W. Norton and Co.

Beck, U. (2007). *Weltrisikogesellschaft*. Frankfurt/M.: Suhrkamp.

Burdack, J. & Hesse, M (2006). Reife, Stagnation oder Wende? Perspektiven zu Suburbanisierung, Post-Suburbia und Zwischenstadt: Ein Überblick zum Stand der Forschung. *Berichte zur deutschen Landeskunde, 80(4)*, pp. 381-399.

David, P. A. (1994). Why are Institutions the 'Carriers of History'? Path Dependence and the Evolution of Conventions, Organizations and Institutions. *Structural Change and Economic Dynamics. 5(2)*, pp. 205-220. doi:10.1016/0954-349X(94)90002-7

Deeg, R. (2001). Institutional Change and the Uses and Limits of Path Dependency: The Case of German Finance. *Discussion Paper 6*. Köln: Max-Planck-Institut für Gesellschaftsforschung. Retrieved from: http://www.mpi-fg-koeln.mpg.de/pu/mpifg_dp/dp01-6.pdf

Fürst, D., Gailing, L., Pollermann, K. & Röhring, A. (eds.) (2008). *Kulturlandschaft als Handlungsraum: Institutionen und Governance im Umgang mit dem regionalen Gemeinschaftsgut Kulturlandschaft*. Dortmund: Rohn.

Garud, R. & Karnøe, P. (2001). Path Creation as a Process of Mindful Deviation. In R. Garud & P. Karnøe (eds.), *Path Dependence and Creation* (pp. 1-38). Mahwah/USA: Lawrence Erlbaum.

Holling, C. S. (1973). Resilience and Stability of Ecological Systems. *Annual Review of Ecology and Systematics, 4*, pp. 1-23. doi: 10.1146/annurev.es.04.110173.000245

Holling, C. S. & Gunderson, L. H. (2002). Resilience and adaptive cycles. In C. S. Holling & L. H. Gunderson (eds.), *Panarchy: Understanding Transformations in Human and Natural Systems* (pp. 25-62). Washington: Island Press.

Kühn, M. & Gailing, L. (2008). From Green Belts to Regional Parks: History and Challenges of Suburban Landscape Planning in Berlin. In M. Amati (ed.), *Urban Green Belts in the Twenty-first Century (Urban Planning and Environment)* (pp. 185-202). Aldershot/Burlington (USA): Ashgate Publishing Limited.

Mayntz, R. (2002). Zur Theoriefähigkeit makro-sozialer Analysen. In R. Mayntz (ed.), *Akteure – Mechanismen – Modelle. Zur Theoriefähigkeit makro-sozialer Analysen* (pp. 7-43). Frankfurt/M.: Campus.

North, D. (1990). *Institutions, Institutional Change and Economic Performance.* Cambridge: Cambridge University Press.

Pierson, P. (2000). Increasing Returns, Path Dependence, and the Study of Politics. *American Political Science Review, 94(2)*, pp. 251-267.

Quast, J. & Ehlert, V. (2005). *Concept ODERBRUCH 2010 as an Example towards Sustainable Multifunctional Use of Polders in the Context of Integrated Land, Water and Flood Management.* Retrieved from: http://www.zalf.de/icid/ICID_ERC2005/HTML/ERC2005PDF/Topic_5/Quast. pdf

Röhring, A. & Gailing, L. (2005). *Institutional problems and management aspects of shared cultural landscapes: Conflicts and possible solutions concerning a common good from a social science perspective* (IRS-Working Paper). Retrieved from: http://www.irs-net.de/download/shared-landscape.pdf

Schreyögg, G., Sydow, J. & Koch, J. (2003). Organisatorische Pfade. Von der Pfadabhängigkeit zur Pfadkreation? In G. Schreyögg & J. Sydow (eds.), *Strategische Prozesse und Pfade* (pp. 257-294). Wiesbaden: Gabler.

Theuvsen, L. (2004). Pfadabhängigkeit als Forschungsprogramm für die Agrarökonomie. *Agrarwirtschaft, 53(3)*, pp. 111-122.

Walker, B., Carpenter, S., Anderies, J., Abel, N., Cumming, G. S., Janssen, M., Lebel, L., Norberg, J., Peterson, G. D. & Pritchard, R. (2002). Resilience management in social-ecological systems: a working hypothesis for a participatory approach. *Conservation Ecology, 6(1)*. Retrieved from: http://www.consecol.org/vol6/iss1/art14/

Walker, B., Holling, C. S., Carpenter, S. R. & Kinzig, A. (2004). Resilience, Adaptability and Transformability in Social-ecological Systems. *Ecology and Society, 9(2)*. Retrieved from: http://www.ecologyandsociety.org/vol9/iss2/art5/

Young, O. (2002). *The Institutional Dimensions of Environmental Change: Fit, Interplay and Scale.* Cambridge (USA): The MIT Press.

Resilience and Resistance of Buildings and Built Structures to Flood Impacts – Approaches to Analysis and Evaluation

Thomas Naumann, Johannes Nikolowski, Sebastian Golz, Reinhard Schinke

1. Introduction

The global increase in the frequency and intensity of natural hazards as well as the rising number of victims and growing damages make the necessity of improved risk reduction at the societal level abundantly clear (UN/ISDR, 2005). We must assume that climate change will continue to exacerbate meteorological events (IPCC, 2007). At the same time, it is clear that the constantly growing intensity of settlements and concentration of material assets in endangered areas are resulting in distinctly heightened vulnerability (Munich Re Group, 2009). In contrast to the dominant perspectives of the past, the scientific, planning and administrative handling of natural hazards is now marked by the insight that complete protection from these risks is neither technically possible nor economically appropriate. As a result, new concepts known as 'risk management' are becoming prevalent; besides the natural hazards, they especially include an analysis of vulnerability as well as the effectiveness and efficiency of protective and precautionary strategies for the potentially affected subjects and objects. In this context, the concepts of 'resilience' and 'resistance' are becoming more important.

Important receptors within endangered built-up areas include buildings with their manifold constructive forms and uses, which is why their vulnerability has a strong effect on economic damage. In case of a natural hazard, these buildings experience periodic pressures through more intensive hazardous events such as flooding, heat waves, heavy rainfall, and hail. Therefore, a part of risk management involves studying the hazard-specific vulnerability of buildings and built structures. Overviews of the vulnerability of buildings, especially to the natural risk of flooding, are given by Roos (2003), Kelman and Spence (2004) as well as Proverbs and Soetanto (2004).

Concept development and the implementation of structural measures to reduce vulnerability can be carried out on the basis of a systematic vulnerability analysis. This paper focuses on both methods of vulnerability analysis and specific measures to reduce the vulnerability of buildings, using the example of flood impacts. We are currently experiencing a paradigm shift, especially in dealing with risks from flooding. In contrast to traditional flood protection measures, which reduce only the probability of a settled area being flooded, integrated concepts that focus on increasing the resilience and resistance of buildings as receptors of floods are increasingly being developed (Ashley, Blanksby, Chapman, & Zhou, 2007).

B. Müller, *German Annual of Spatial Research and Policy 2010*,
German Annual of Spatial Research and Policy,
DOI 10.1007/978-3-642-12785-4_9, © Springer-Verlag Berlin Heidelberg 2011

2.   Overall Methodology

2.1 The Vulnerability of Building Types

The causal relationships regarding the development of flood risks for urban land uses are described by the generic 'Source-Pathway-Receptor-Consequence' concept (ICE, 2001). According to this concept, meteorological events (source) encounter an object or subject (receptor) via a flood wave spreading (pathway). Depending on the characteristics of the receptor and additional conditions, this results in more or less severe negative consequences, for example damages to buildings and their inventories that can be monetarized. Thus, the flood risk depends on:

- The meteorological influences ("sources") and hydrological-hydraulic conditions ("pathways"),
- The exposure of the receptors,
- The characteristics of receptors and additional conditions (vulnerability).

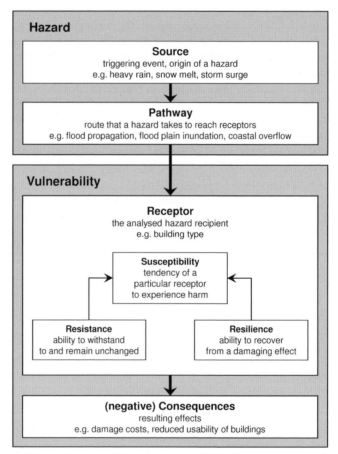

Fig. 1: Source-Pathway-Receptor-Consequence concept with specifications of the receptor. Source: ICE (2001).

Quantifying the vulnerability of receptors exposed to hazardous events is an elementary component of determining both risks and the effectiveness of precautionary measures. Numerous definitions have been developed to describe the term vulnerability (Thywissen, 2006). Three characteristics of vulnerability can be discerned, following Schanze (2010): susceptibility, value or function, and coping capacity. Susceptibility characterizes the degree to which an element or system at risk reacts to the pressure of the hazardous event, while value or function and coping capacity have decisive influence on the (negative) consequences of a natural hazard.

From an engineering perspective, the focus is on the susceptibility of buildings due to flooding, since buildings are significant receptors in cities and regions of developed countries. In case of a hazardous event, varying intensities of damages to buildings can be identified, due to a large variety of processes and mechanisms causing physical damage. Monetary damage refers to the characteristic of value or function, specifying the costs arising from the physical impacts which have occurred. The susceptibility of buildings is affected by their structural design and the materials used. The vulnerability of buildings, therefore, depends on their resistance and/or resilience (see Fig.1). Two principles can be differentiated:

- Resistance: The ability to withstand an impact without relevant changes to the system's status,
- Resilience: The ability to recover from a damaging effect (e.g., reconstruction of buildings).

2.2 The Vulnerability Analysis Approach

This paper presents a synthetic approach to the vulnerability analysis of building types. The main objective of the approach is to determine the amount of damage resulting from specific parameters of a flood event, such as the depth of inundation and flow velocity, and to visualize them employing damage functions. The development and application of damage curves aggregated in different ways to calculate flood-related damages to buildings has been established worldwide (Penning-Rowsell & Chatterton, 1977; Veerbeek & Zevenbergen, 2009; Middelmann-Fernandes, 2010). The vulnerability analysis approach consists of four main components:

- The spatial identification and systematization of building types,
- The analysis of characteristic types of damages that occur to representatives of building types,
- The identification of technically correct refurbishment techniques including the cost parameters,
- The building type-specific derivation of synthetic depth-damage functions.

The first step of vulnerability analysis is based on a semiautomatic, GIS-assisted identification of urban structure types using data from remote sensing and aerial photography. With the aid of field investigations, the identified urban structure types are assigned to building age groups. Building types can be derived by linking

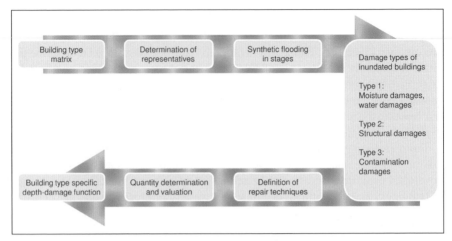

Fig. 2: The synthetic calculation process of flood damages to buildings. Source: Naumann, Nikolowski, and Golz (2009).

the urban structure types with the building age groups. An area-specific building typology can then be used in a study area to differentiate and document the stock of residential buildings, which initially appears very variegated, in a targeted fashion.

In a second step, relevant types of damage to the building stock of building types that can occur because of flood events are systematically assigned to the three characteristic damage types: moisture and water damage, structural damage, or contamination. The intensity and extent of damage can vary widely, depending on the type of damage. For each relevant building type, characteristic representative buildings are selected, analyzed, and documented regarding the details of their geometry, structural design, technical infrastructure, and uses.

In a third step, these representative buildings are flooded virtually, using defined inundation levels (Naumann, Nikolowski, & Golz, 2009). The defined inundation levels help to delineate significant areas for repairing the flood damage to the building. The term "repair" in this context includes both immediate measures to mitigate damage to the building and repairs of the built structures for the long term, for example repairing or replacing structural elements. Then, the costs of refurbishment after a flood event are calculated, based on specifications that document the required repairs for each inundation level. For the most part, the cost estimates employed follow the relevant literature on refurbishment planning.

In a fourth step, the building-type-specific synthetic depth-damage functions are derived to obtain the major result of the vulnerability analysis. The course of the function shows the ratio between the inundation levels and the corresponding repair costs (Fig. 3).

Either quality-assured damage appraisals or detailed cost determinations of long-term and technically correct repairs after a flood event are necessary in order to validate synthetic depth-damage functions. It should be mentioned in this context that the methods for developing synthetic depth-damage functions and the content

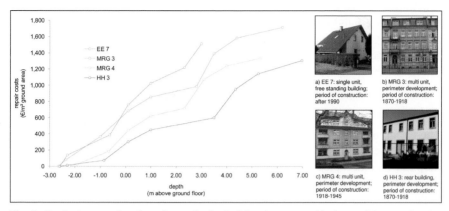

Fig. 3: Depth-damage functions for particular building types considering moisture and water damage. Source: Naumann, Nikolowski, and Golz (2009) (modified).

structure of damage appraisals are comparable, since both are founded upon a description of damages, the definition of required repair techniques, and the organization of this information in a list of specifications, as well as a calculation of costs.

3. Vulnerability Mitigation Measures

3.1 The Classification and Description of Measures

When the cause-and-effect relationships between flood events and receptors are known, the main prerequisites for developing and assessing preventive measures are at hand. In this context, measures include above all direct interventions in the structural fabric of the buildings that can diminish the extent of damage (Olfert & Schanze, 2007). When classifying such measures, three types can be discerned, in line with the definition of vulnerability mentioned above (Fig. 4; cf. DKKV, 2003).

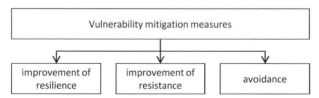

Fig. 4: Classification of measures to reduce vulnerability. Source: Compiled by the authors (2010).

In the following article, fundamental options for reducing the vulnerability of buildings to damage will be explained in terms of these three types of measures. The appropriateness of measures depends on both the original state of the building type and the interrelationships between the building materials and the structural design. For example, using water-resistant materials makes sense only if it ensures that the entire building component or structure is water-resistant as well. When deriving suitable measures, both the different possibilities for existing buildings and for ones to be newly built are taken into account as well as the structural features of the various building types.

The Improvement of Resilience

The design of resilient built structures and conception of appropriate constructive forms focuses on reducing the extent of damage when buildings are flooded so that they can be reoccupied quickly and at low cost. In contrast to resistant systems, where efforts are made to work 'against the water' and to keep it away from the building, the objective of designing resilient systems is to 'live with the water'. Using waterproof or water-insensitive materials, integrating them in a goal-oriented manner to achieve resilient structural layers, and combining such measures sensibly when designing various structural elements of a building is a complex task. It requires holistic planning on the part of specialist engineers (Wingfield, Bell, & Bowker, 2005; Bowker, Escarameia, & Tagg, 2007). Important structural parameters include, for example, water penetration resistance, resistance to water vapor transmission, or porosity, which contribute decisively to the drying properties of types of building material. The various measures must be differentiated according to the building materials and the structural design employed in order to obtain a long-lasting and durable structure (Garvin, Reid, & Scott, 2005). Similarly, improving building resilience also includes moving vulnerable elements to higher stories.

The Improvement of Resistance

Measures that prevent or delay the penetration of water permanently or temporarily are used to improve resistance during flood events (Bowker et al., 2007). Installing temporary measures, for example mobile stop logs for barring entrances to buildings, requires sufficient advance warning as well as knowledge about proper mounting. In addition, continuous financial expenditures are required for erecting, storing, and maintaining temporary protective systems. In contrast, stationary measures do not require any particular preparation. However, they should be planned so that they do not interfere with the building's normal use.

In particular measures conceptualized during the design phase of new buildings result in enhanced resistance. Important parameters for design include, for example, the potential duration and the maximum depth of flooding; due to different water depths inside and outside a building, critical buoyant forces and hydrostatic compressive forces can impact the structure. Improving the resistance of an existing building is problematic, on the other hand, as a horizontal sealing of the basement floor that will be reliable long-term can be installed only with substantial interventions in the building structure. Temporarily closing openings such as basement windows and entrances to buildings can enhance resistance only if the stability of the exterior wall structure is not put at risk.

Avoidance

Avoidance measures regarding the building as a receptor include, above all, measures that result in elevation of the site of the building by creating an embankment or by mounting the building on pillars. In addition, designing and erecting new buildings without cellars is also considered avoidance. These measures will not be examined more closely in the following article.

3.2 The Selection, Ex-ante Analysis, and Comparison of Measures

The vulnerability analysis described above can be used to select suitable preventive measures, to analyze their impacts ex ante, and to compare them with alternative measures. It is helpful in particular for deciding between measures to improve resistance or resilience. Fig. 5 expands the SPRC concept shown in Fig. 1 by including implementation of the relevant measures.

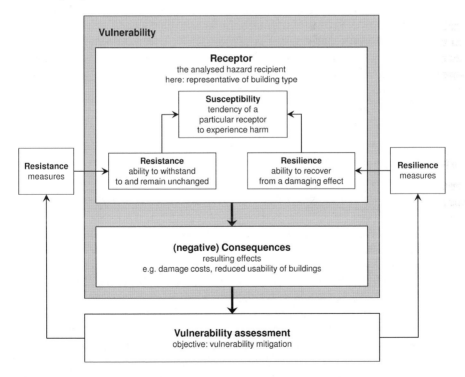

Fig. 5: Iterative vulnerability assessment considering different resilience and resistance measures. Source: Compiled by the authors (2010).

The vulnerability analysis can be employed in Fig. 5 as follows:
• The analysis of the vulnerability of a representative example of a building type its original state,

- A review of the suitability of resistance, resilience, and avoidance measures, taking the flooding characteristics and the built structure of the representative example into account,
- The development or definition of technically suitable and reliable measures to enhance resistance and resilience,
- An analysis of the vulnerability of the representative example in its altered state,
- A comparison of alternative measures or combinations of measures regarding their efficiency.

Fig. 6 shows the qualitative changes in the course of the depth-damage function for the "vulnerability mitigation measures". In Fig. 6a, the effects of measures that enhance the resilience of buildings are characterized by the function's diminished slope. The course of the function in Fig. 6b shows a reduction of damages due to flooding up to a defined depth by means of measures to enhance resistance. However, when the defined depth of flooding (the so-called intake threshold) is exceeded, the effects of the measure are lost. Fig. 6c illustrates how avoidance works with the changed starting point of the damage function (Δ), resulting in lesser damages at the same depth.

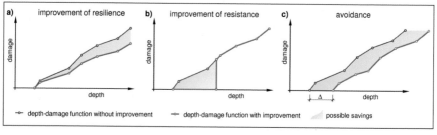

Fig. 6: The qualitative influence of mitigation measures on the depth-damage function. Source: Compiled by the authors (2008).

Thanks to the detailed description of damages ranging from the building as an entire system down to structural details, it is also possible to examine combinations of measures. This can help to achieve an optimal reduction of the extent of damage. Fig. 7 shows a possible qualitative course of a depth-damage function by combining resilience measures, resistance measures, and avoidance measures. Erecting a building without a basement, for example, shifts the entire function to the right. If measures to enhance resilience are taken into account, the function also slopes upwards less, and implementing measures to increase resistance defines a depth of flooding up to which only lesser damages occur.

4.   The Evaluation of Vulnerability Mitigation Measures

When evaluating vulnerability mitigation measures, numerous economic aspects must be taken into account, such as the points in time when analysis and

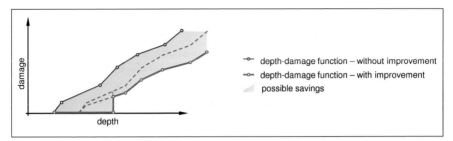

Fig. 7: An example of combining vulnerability mitigation measures in terms of resistance, resilience and avoidance. Source: Compiled by the authors (2008).

implementation are carried out, the capital investment costs, the required costs for maintenance and repairs, the lifespan of the existing and modified elements, as well as the possible extent of damage and the regularity with which the relevant impacts occur.

The point in time when vulnerability mitigation measures are implemented is closely related to the condition of the building and the present value of the structural component in question. As a matter of principle, the optimal time for integrating such measures is when a building is being planned or is under construction. In the case of existing buildings, economically advantageous conditions arise if the measures can be integrated when repairs after a damaging event are carried out, or during regular replacement or necessary maintenance of building components (Fig. 8). This approach permits one to consider the capital investment costs of the measure as merely being additional costs, so that economically acceptable solutions can be found more easily in this way (BWG, 2004).

Linking the regularity with which the observed impact occurs with the synthetic inundation levels enables one to select and include vulnerability mitigation measures, taking their effects on the damage function as well as their cost effectiveness into account. As a result, a solution acceptable both in economic and in structural terms can be derived for the concrete location of a building or a building type in a flood-prone area.

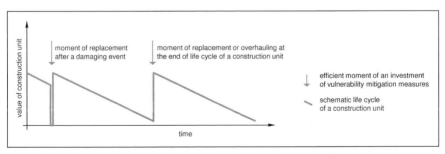

Fig. 8: The schematic life cycle of a building component with economically suitable times for integrating vulnerability mitigation measures in existing buildings. Source: Compiled by the authors (2010).

5. Conclusions

The paper outlines how the hazard-specific vulnerability of characteristic building types can be analyzed ex ante by employing an engineering approach. This approach includes both the systematic analysis of the vulnerability of building types and the classification and quantification of potential negative effects. This synthetic approach is explained in more detail, using flood impacts as an example. In principle, the method of vulnerability analysis presented here is also applicable to other hazardous events, such as heavy rains or heat waves, due to its flexibility and adaptability to changed boundary conditions. Targeted measures to enhance the resistance and resilience of buildings and structural elements can be developed, and their efficiency can be assessed, on the basis of such vulnerability analyses. The vulnerability approach, based on engineering knowledge, creates an important basis for analyzing the risks of land uses in cities and regions in terms of natural hazards.

References

Ashley, R., Blanksby, J., Chapman, J. & Zhou J. (2007). Towards integrated approaches to reduce flood risk in urban areas. In R. Ashley, S. Garvin, E. Pasche, A. Vassilopoulos & C. Zevenbergen (eds.), *Advances in urban flood management*. London: Taylor & Francis.

Bowker, P., Escarameia, M. & Tagg, A. (2007). *Improving the flood performance of new buildings – Flood resilient construction* (Guidance produced by a consortium of CIRIA, HR Wallingford, Leeds Metropolitan University, WRe and Waterman Group). London: RIBA Publishing.

BWG – Bundesamt für Wasser und Geologie (ed.) (2004). Hochwasservorsorge – Erkenntnisse aus vier Fallbeispielen. *Berichte des BWG, Serie Wasser, Nr. 6*. Bern: Bundesamt für Wasser und Geologie.

DKKV – Deutsches Komitee für Katastrophenvorsorge e.V. (ed.) (2003). Hochwasservorsorge in Deutschland – Lernen aus der Katastrophe 2002 im Elbegebiet. *Schriftenreihe des DKKV, Heft 29*. Bonn: DKKV.

Garvin, S., Reid, J. & Scott, M. (2005). Standards for the repair of buildings following flooding. *CIRIA publication, C623*. London: CIRIA.

ICE – Institution of Civil Engineers (2001). *Learning to Live with Rivers. Final Report of the ICE's Presidential Commission the Review the Technical Aspects of Flood Risk Management in England and Wales*. Retrieved from: www.ice.org.uk/rtfpdf/iceflooding.pdf

IPCC – Intergovernmental Panel on Climate Change (2007). Climate Change 2007: Impacts, Adaptation and Vulnerability. In M. L. Parry, O. F. Canziani, J. P. Palutikof, P. J. van der Linden & C. E. Han-son (eds.), *Contribution of Working Group II to the Fourth Assessment Report of the Intergovernmental Panel on Climate Change*. Cambridge (UK)/New York (USA): Cambridge University Press.

Kelman, I. & Spence, R. (2004). An overview of flood actions on buildings. *Engineering Geology, 73*, pp. 297-309.

Middelmann-Fernandes, M. H. (2010). Flood damage estimation beyond stage-damage functions – An Australian example. *Journal of Flood Risk Management, 3*, pp. 88–96.

Munich Re Group – Münchener Rückversicherungs-Gesellschaft (2009). *Topics Geo, Naturkatastrophen 2008 – Analysen, Bewertungen, Positionen*. München: Munich ReGroup.

Naumann, T., Nikolowski, J. & Golz, S. (2009). Synthetic depth-damage functions – A detailed tool for analysing flood resilience of building types. In E. Pasche, N. Evelpidou, C. Zevenbergen, R. Ashley & S. Garvin (eds.), *Road map towards a flood resilient urban environment*. Hamburg: Institut für Wasserbau der TUHH.

Olfert, A. & Schanze, J. (2007). Methodology for ex-post evaluation of measures and instruments for flood risk reduction. *FLOODsite Consortium Report, T12-07-01*. Retrieved from: www.floodsite.net

Penning-Rowsell, E. C. & Chatterton, J. B. (1977). *The benefits of flood alleviation – A manual of assessment techniques (The blue manual)*. Aldershot, Hampshire: Gower Technical Press.

Proverbs, D. G. & Soetanto, R. (2004) *Flood damaged property: a guide to repair*. Oxford (UK): Blackwell Publishing.

Roos, I. W. (2003). Damage to buildings. *Delft Cluster Publication, DC1-233-9*. Delft: DUP Standard.

Schanze, J. (2010). Flood risk management – basic understanding and integrated methodologies. In J. Schanze (ed.), *Methodologies for Integrated Flood Risk Management – Research Advances at European Pilot Sites*. CRC Press/Balkema: Leiden (forthcoming).

Thywissen, K. (2006). *Components of risk – A comparative glossary*. United Nations University Institute for Environment and Human Security (UNU-EHS), Bonn. Retrieved from: http://www.ehs.unu.edu/article:217

UN/ISDR – United Nation International Strategy for Disaster Reduction (2005). *Hyogo Framework for Action 2005-2015: Building the Resilience of Nations and Communities to Disasters*. Retrieved from: www.unisdr.org.

Veerbeek, W. & Zevenbergen, C. (2009). Deconstructing urban food damages – Increasing the expressiveness of flood damage models combining a high level of detail with a broad attribute set. *Journal of Flood Risk Management, 2*, pp. 45-57.

Wingfield, J., Bell, M. & Bowker, P. (2005). *Improving the flood resilience of buildings through improved materials, methods and details* (CIRIA publication SC04006). London: CIRIA.

Planning for Risk Reduction and Organizing for Resilience in the Context of Natural Hazards

Gérard Hutter

1. Introduction

Contributions to current debates about dealing with natural hazards increasingly refer to both notions of planning and resilience. For instance, some authors argue that reducing the risk related to natural hazards in the context of climate change requires long-term planning and resilience to deal with a high degree of uncertainty (e.g., Overbeck, Hartz, & Fleischhauer, 2008; Müller & Hutter, 2009). Other scholars who use the concept of resilience tend to be rather distant to notions of planning, especially long-term planning (e.g., Weick & Sutcliffe, 2007). They argue that effective problem solving through planning and implementation is a rare case under real-world conditions and that organizations preoccupied with planning are ill-prepared for uncertain futures.

The notions of planning and resilience have both multiple meanings (e.g., see Alexander, 2000; Bryson, 2004; Wiechmann (2008) for (spatial) planning; Wildavsky, 1991; Folke et al., 2002; Sutcliffe & Vogus, 2003; Brand & Jax, 2007; Berkes (2007) for resilience). Up to now, no overall framework exists with regard to understanding the complex relationships between planning and resilience in order to deal with natural hazards within the context of urban development. In this paper, no attempt is made to provide an overall synthesis based on a comprehensive analysis of the diverse literature about planning and resilience. This paper has a rather narrow conceptual purpose. It is written from an organizational perspective (with regard to the literature used, e.g., Van de Ven & Poole, 1995; Weick & Sutcliffe, 2007; as well as with reference to the object of inquiry in the social world). It seeks to make a contribution of modest scale to ongoing debates through focusing on organizations in the public sector (e.g., state authorities or local government and administration). The paper develops some conceptual guidance for the empirical analysis of organizations that acknowledge the differences between planning for risk reduction and organizing for resilience, and that seek to combine the two social processes because they are both important for dealing with natural hazards.

In Section 2, planning for risk reduction is conceptualized as a specific success and future-oriented social process at the group level. In contrast, organizing for resilience is conceptualized as a failure-oriented social process of groups within organizations. Section 3 argues that both planning for risk reduction and organizing for resilience are likely to develop in organizations, but in different ways. This section elucidates on four possible ways in some detail. In Section 4, conclusions are drawn.

B. Müller, *German Annual of Spatial Research and Policy 2010*,
German Annual of Spatial Research and Policy,
DOI 10.1007/978-3-642-12785-4_10, © Springer-Verlag Berlin Heidelberg 2011

2. Comparing Planning for Risk Reduction and Organizing for Resilience in Groups

Characterizing planning solely through its temporal reference to the future is not sufficient for gaining a useful concept of planning for risk reduction. Everyday life is characterized by its continuous reference to the future in terms of 'a tomorrow'. In contrast to daily life, planning is characterized by formulating well-defined decision premises for future decisions in terms of goals, actions, measures, and resource allocations for realizing goals (Van de Ven & Poole, 1995; Wiechmann, 2008). Organizations define criteria for what counts as future success and how this success can be realized through deploying resources for specific actions and measures. They are motivated to act through envisioning a future state of success in specific context conditions. Planning for risk reduction in particular refers to a social process in which a like-minded group of persons within an organization is able to envision a future state of affairs that is characterized by an acceptable risk compared to the current state of their situation. This means that risk (Schanze (2006) defined it as the product of the probability of an occurrence of negative consequences) is anticipated to decide to what extent and how risk can be reduced through various measures and actions. Apart from its close relationship to future decisions and visions of success, planning is characterized by its attempt to use a set of well-defined, especially (mutually) exclusive categories for considering specific measures and actions and their consequences (Mintzberg, 1994; Weick & Sutcliffe, 2007). This picture of planning is consistent with the argument that organizations that favor planning will try to explain stress, crisis, and even disaster through failures in planning and/or implementation – in contrast to explanations that underline the limitations of planning in an uncertain world. Of course, "after the fact, it is easy to say, that whatever happened should have been prevented" (Wildavsky, 1991, p. 220). This will lead organizations convinced of the merits of planning to search for failures in planning and implementation processes and to argue for more control in dealing with natural hazards and/or for learning-oriented approaches to planning through continuous evaluation and revisions of planning procedures, methods, and plans (Carroll, Rudolph, & Hatakenaka, 2003). One great advantage of planning for risk reduction is that it focuses the attention of organizations on issues that can be explicitly communicated (e.g., statements in plan documents, methods).

With regard to process, planning for risk reduction resembles the teleological process theory of change (Van de Ven & Poole, 1995) in which organizations are dissatisfied with the present state of their situation ('unacceptable risk') and search for new information to analyze and evaluate their current state of affairs. Based on these activities, they are able to construct a goal for risk reduction that is supported by at least a majority of organizational members to ensure goal realization through plan implementation. However, this ideal-type description of planning as a teleological process of change does acknowledge that internal and external constraints make easy plan implementation difficult and rather unlikely. Therefore, further rounds of dissatisfaction, searching, goal formulation, and implementation are likely.

Organizations that plan are strong in creating a precise 'picture' of a willed future or in constructing multiple futures through scenario planning. Planning can then resemble a dynamic process in terms of a self-fulfilling prophecy. Having a plan makes people within organizations confident about the effectiveness of the chosen course of (planned) action which leads – under specific context conditions – to tangible action that confirms the initial expectations embedded in the plan. Planning can be used to focus the attention of a group of people on common issues, to ensure their participation in the planning process, to gather information about important issues, to schedule activities, and, finally, to set the agenda for action (Mintzberg, 1994). However strong planning and the context conditions that support it may

Dimension	Planning for Risk Reduction	Organizing for Resilience
Content	Success as envisioned through social goal construction	Failures as consequences of assumptions and related values and norms
	Set of well-defined categories that are used in a consistent way	New categories to consider new details of context
	Explanation of stress, crisis, and disaster through specific failures of planning and/or implementation	Explanation of stress, crisis, and disaster through systemic relationships of technology, culture, people
	Set of specific actions and measures as well as knowledge and information about specific consequences	Broad repertoire of measures and actions as well as knowledge about possible consequences
Process	People are dissatisfied with the present state of affairs ('unacceptable risk')	People scan the present situation to identify failures as quickly as possible
	Search process leads to information about possible goals, measures, and actions	Failure analysis is based on conceptual slack and respectful interaction; blaming is avoided
	People construct a goal for risk reduction ('goal consensus')	Experts swiftly decide about an appropriate response and are ready to revise decisions
	Measures are deployed and actions are undertaken to implement the goal	Monitoring of events due to internal and/or external conditions
Context	Ability to consider formal institutions and related expectations	Ability to consider learning as a core value and complex ongoing process
	Learning culture that supports plan formulation, implementation, and evaluation	Learning culture that supports learning from failure (e.g., 'near misses')

Tab. 1: Comparing and contrasting planning for risk reduction and organizing for resilience at the level of groups. Source: Based on Van de Ven & Poole (1995); Wiechmann (2008) to understand planning; Weick & Sutcliffe (2001, 2007); Sutcliffe & Vogus (2003); Sitkin (1996) in order to consider organizing for resilience.

be, there are limits to it (e.g., Weick & Sutcliffe, 2007). Planning makes sense if strong expectations in terms of plan premises and plans are based on broad and valid knowledge and a source of information about past, present, and future context conditions. Confident planners are able to consider complex context conditions when creating elaborate and complex plans (e.g., contingency planning, scenario planning). Organizations or groups that acknowledge the limits of valid knowledge and information about the future states of context will start to complement their decisions and planned actions through efforts to organize for resilience (Tab. 1).

Hollnagel understands resilience as some form of control of organizations in unstable, complex, and uncertain contexts. In contrast to planning for risk reduction, resilience is the ability of an organization (or other social entity like a group) to deal with the negative consequences of hazards that have already happened (Weick & Sutcliffe, 2007, p. 68). "The essence of resilience is therefore the intrinsic ability of an organization (system) to maintain or regain a dynamically stable state, which allows it to continue operations after a major mishap and/or in the presence of continuous stress" (Hollnagel, 2006, p. 16). An assessment of resilience is then based on two judgments (Sutcliffe & Vogus, 2003, p. 95): Firstly, an organization or organizational unit faces a major mishap or continuous stress (a judgment that a hazard or threat is present); secondly, an organization is able to continue operations in accordance with some performance expectations despite the fact that a 'collapse' or significant decline in performance is highly probable (judgment of 'doing ok' in accordance with some criteria for performance). This understanding of resilience can be elaborated upon by looking at different components of resilience (Weick & Sutcliffe, 2007, p. 71). Components of resilience are the:

- Ability to absorb strain and preserve the ability to function despite the presence of continuous stress and/or a major mishap (see discussion so far),
- Ability to recover or bounce back from a major mishap and/or continuous stress as the system becomes better able to absorb surprises and 'stretch' rather than collapse,
- Ability to learn and grow from previous episodes of resilient action (Sutcliffe & Vogus 2003, p. 108).

"Resilience is short on specific promises; adversity may be overcome, but exactly how remains unspecified in advance" (Wildavsky, 1991, p. 121). How then can organizations consider resilience as an ability to organize for?

Tab. 1 suggests that people who organize as a group of like-minded people interested in resilience focus on the following contents and processes. The most distinctive feature is that group members are preoccupied with failure and not success (Weick & Sutcliffe, 2007). "A strategy of resilience does not mean waiting for a disease to strike before trying to respond to it. Rather, it means preparing for the inevitable – the appearance of a new, surprising disease – by expanding general knowledge and technical facility, and generalized command over resources" (Wildavsky, 1991, p. 221). Failure (or in the words of Wildavsky a "surprising disease") is seen less as being simple deviations from existing norms and rules, but as being due to existing assumptions and related values, norms, and goals that implicitly or explicitly guide expectation-building. Failure analysis is more cognitive than in the case of simply detecting, reaffirming, and correcting deviating behavior from existing values, norms, and goals. Therefore, one further distinctive feature of organizing for resilience is that resilient people within organizations seek to create new categories for (subjectively) new details of contexts that have been 'overlooked' up to now or are new due to significantly changed context conditions within an organization. Furthermore, they have a more conceptually elaborated and at the same time more detailed knowledge base than non-resilient people due to more experience with the unexpected, specialized memory skills, and an ongoing interest in learning in order to expand knowledge beyond what is currently known. This corresponds to the assumption that resilient organizational members are more willing to explain stress, crisis, and disaster through systemic relationships between technologies, people, cultures, and unknown features of organizations and context conditions than through a narrow focus on a specific process like planning. One further feature of organizing for resilience is that scanning (or perception) and the interpretation of hazards are closely and mutually linked to the spectrum of action possibilities of individual group members as well as the group as a whole social system within an organization (Sutcliffe & Vogus, 2003; Weick & Sutcliffe, 2007). Context conditions that people can act upon are more likely to be perceived and interpreted as circumstances that require more attention than conditions for which perceived appropriate action possibilities are lacking. The range of scanning interpretation possibilities on the one hand and the range of action abilities grow together, if resources in terms of attention, time, money, and social resources are available.

From a process and development perspective, resilience is not necessarily a fixed quality that resembles some kind of "super material" (Sutcliffe & Vogus, 2003). It is less a category and more a dimension of organizing. However, just how groups and organizations develop towards highly resilient systems is still unexplored (Sutcliffe & Vogus, 2003). What can be seen as a plausible starting point is the assumption that groups that organize for resilience are more interested in present functioning than in organizing for an envisioned 'positive future' in terms of social goal construction. The goal of organizing for resilience is more a means to understand current weak points of organizing than to focus attention mainly on the future, as in the case of planning for risk reduction. Three features of organizing illustrate the point: Firstly, group members scan present conditions continuously to identify possible failures as quickly as possible. This facilitates containing the consequences of failure (Weick & Sutcliffe, 2007). Secondly, failure analysis requires that people with different experiences, cultural backgrounds, analytical perspectives, and knowledge are involved. However, failure analysis only leads to contextually sensitive and sometimes radically new insights if group members constantly interact, based on self-respect and appreciation for the reports and contributions of others (Weick & Sutcliffe, 2007). Thirdly, using the verb 'organizing' instead of the noun 'organization' also means that groups are willing and collectively able to revise decisions about goals, actions, and measures if new, more convincing evidence is available and/or interpretations are further developed in changing context conditions.

Being preoccupied with failure is difficult and unlikely under context conditions that promote people who are preoccupied with realizing planned success (Sitkin, 1996). Furthermore, organizing for resilience is based not only on attention to failure, but also on success in dealing with major mishaps or continuous stress (Sutcliffe & Vogus, 2003). Therefore, this paper argues that organizing for resilience requires ongoing attention to possible failure and failure analysis in an organizational learning context that supports these group processes as preconditions for effectively dealing with hazards in general, and natural hazards in particular.

Four ways	The overall direction for combining planning for risk reduction and organizing for resilience in an organization
Accept both processes	Members of the organization acknowledge and discuss the advantages and disadvantages of both planning for risk reduction and organizing for resilience; they seek to develop strategies that are a at the same time robust and flexible. A discourse about planning and resilience is to some extent decoupled from arenas for decisions and actions.
Temporal separation	An organization dominated by planning for risk reduction changes to a dominant logic of organizing for resilience after a major mishap, crisis, or disaster ('punctuated equilibrium'). Organizations that organize for resilience resemble so-called 'High Reliability Organizations (HRO)'.
'Spatial' separation	A group within an organization develops a planning approach that is capable of preparing for 'intelligent failure' (Sitkin, 1996); alternatively, one group specializes in planning for risk reduction and another group specializes in resilience, the two groups continuously interact with each other based on respect and open communication.
Synthesis	An organization develops in the direction of a 'learning organization' capable of learning from experience through 'open' and 'deep learning' (Carroll et al. 2003). Organizations are able to solve problems in expanding the learning portfolio through a strong commitment to learning as a core value.

Tab. 2: Four ways of combining planning for risk reduction and organizing for resilience in organizations. Source: Based on Poole & Van de Ven (1989).

3. Planning for Risk Reduction and Organizing for Resilience in Organizations

An organization is a specific form of social system that is characterized by explicit rules of membership (e.g., a working contract as a precondition of membership), a formal hierarchy of positions and competencies, as well as multiple goals and stakeholders (Aldrich & Ruef, 2006; especially the latter holds true in the public sector, Bryson 2004). In Germany, organizations in the public sector have specific responsibilities for dealing with natural hazards. For instance, in principle, state authorities and local government have the responsibility to protect people and their property from being negatively affected by flooding (Hutter, 2007). However, the exact form of responsibility is not fixed over time, but can change due to political, financial, and further conditions. Planning practices are also changing. Based on surveys and case studies, Selle (2005) concludes that spatial planning practices at the local level in Germany are highly diverse and that planners try to consider the limitations of planning due to political constraints and manifold uncertainties in context conditions. Hence, concepts that point to the limits of planning, like organizing for resilience, could be welcome in organizations responsible for spatial planning (Overbeck et al., 2008). This paper suggests that organizations can combine planning for risk reduction and organizing for resilience in different ways (see Tab. 2). The four ways of combining the two social processes are presented as a guide to empirical analysis, not as rigid models of organizational change and development.

Accept both processes and use them constructively

A first step towards actively combining planning and resilience lies in affirming discursively that both social processes and related contents are important for organizations in the public sector. In line with this, Kuhlicke and Kruse (2009) argue that considering anticipation/planning and resilience requires first and foremost a public discourse about strategies for dealing with natural hazards which are robust in the face of partly known and unknown (future) context conditions and at the same time flexible enough to deal with radical surprise.

Temporal separation – take time into account

The first way is characterized to some extent through inconsistencies (e.g., open conversation in an organization about planning and resilience on the one hand, and organized action that is based primarily on plans on the other). A more consistency-oriented approach is developed when organizations deal with both processes through temporal separation. In this case, planning for risk reduction is the dominant logic of an organization in phase one, whereas phase two can be described as being characterized by an overall approach for dealing with natural hazards through organizing for resilience. Organizations that consequently adopt the ideas put forth by Weick and Sutcliffe (2007) for 'Managing the Unexpected' will follow a dominant logic of dealing with complex and uncertain context conditions through preoccupation with failure, reluctance to simplify interpretation, commitment to resilience, and deference to expertise (not status or formal authority). It remains an open question, however, about which organizations will undergo this radical change from being preoccupied with planning to enthusiastically organizing for resilience (Sutcliffe & Vogus, 2003). This could especially hold true for the public sector.

`Spatial´ separation – clarify levels of analysis

Due to institutional constraints, it can be expected that public sector organizations will sometimes be forced to avoid radical change in order not to disappoint important stakeholders. In this case, new solutions have to be integrated into existing internal context conditions of organizations. Spatial separation means that social levels for different social processes are clarified – hence, the term 'spatial' is used in a metaphorical way. Clarifying levels can mean at least two things: Firstly, one social process, like planning for risk reduction, is interpreted as a dominant process in organizations, whereas the second process, organizing for resilience, is used to continuously reflect the limits of this process of dealing with uncertain context conditions. Some planners may even plan for 'intelligent failure' (Sitkin, 1996) to expand the range of what is known at a certain point in time. Intelligent failures are characterized, among others (Sitkin, 1996, pp. 554-556), by 'well-planned actions', 'uncertain outcomes', modest outcome scale', and 'domain relevance'. Secondly, 'spatial' separation could mean that different organizational units (groups) within one overall organizational structure specialize in planning for risk reduction and organizing for resilience. For instance, local officials responsible for spatial planning specialize in planning for risk reduction through reducing damage potentials in flood-prone areas whereas officials responsible for environmental protection are more concerned about resilient approaches to dealing with natural hazards based on their understanding of ecological resilience (see Hutter, 2007).

Synthesis – introduce new terms

Dealing with different social processes by temporal or level analysis leaves each set of assumptions and characteristics basically intact (Poole & Van de Ven, 1989, p. 567). Both planning for risk reduction and organizing for resilience are assumed to be fundamentally sound. However, it is also possible that new terms and concepts can be introduced to gain a new perspective on the problem of combining different social processes in organizations. This paper, however, does not attempt to introduce a new term or concept for combining planning for risk reduction and organizing for resilience to deal with natural hazards. One reason for this is that new concepts and terms can be rather vague if they have been introduced without empirical evidence about their (possible) existence. Consider the example of the 'learning organization' (Carroll et al., 2003). Carroll and colleagues suggest that organizations learn in stages beginning with narrow-minded 'local learning', proceeding to 'controlled learning' based on standards, exact criteria, guidelines, and a complex set of rules, and 'open learning' to foster talk and discussion about options for strategy making, finally developing the motivation and abilities to decide and act as a 'learning organization'. However, the final stage of being a learning organization is more a normative concept without showing evidence that an organization preoccupied with local or controlled learning can actually reach such a development stage. Until this evidence is shown, less ambitious arguments (such as showing how levels of analysis can be clarified) are more useful in empirical work on planning for risk reduction and organizing for resilience in public sector organizations.

4. Conclusion

Up to now, resilience has often been treated as some kind of generic concept (e.g., Wildavsky, 1991; Weick & Sutcliffe, 2007; see also Kuhlicke & Kruse, 2009). In contrast, this paper argues that actor and context-specific conditions are essential for conceptualizing planning for risk reduction and organizing for resilience. Concepts that cover very different types of actors (e.g., state authorities, local government and administration, non-profit organizations) and contexts (e.g., before, during, and after a natural hazard with severe consequences) should be avoided. Even in one organization, like local administration, context conditions can differ sharply between organizational departments (e.g., an office for spatial planning and an office for environmental protection in Dresden, see Hutter, 2007). If we cannot find resilience in reality, this may be due to the fact that important context conditions and related social processes have been overlooked. Resilience in organizations accustomed to planning and plans may be present in how decision makers interpret their plans for dealing with natural hazards and how they develop them further. Planners may even plan for 'intelligent failure' (Sitkin, 1996). The context-specific dynamics of planning and resilience in organizations need to be given much more attention in both research and practice.

References

Aldrich, H. E. & Ruef, M. (2006). *Organizations Evolving*. London/Thousand Oaks: Sage.

Alexander, E. R. (2000). Rationality Revisited: Planning Paradigms in a Post-Postmodernist Perspective. *Journal of Planning Education and Research, vol. 19*, pp. 242-256.

Berkes, F. (2007). Understanding Uncertainty and Reducing Vulnerability: Lessons from Resilience Thinking. *Natural Hazards, vol. 41*, pp. 283-295.

Brand, F. S. & Jax, K. (2007). Focusing the Meaning(s) of Resilience: Resilience as a Descriptive Concept and a Boundary Object. *Ecology and Society, vol. 12, no. 1*.

Bryson, J. M. (2004). *Strategic Planning for Public and Nonprofit Organizations. A Guide to Strengthening and Sustaining Organizational Achievement*. San Francisco: Jossey-Bass.

Carroll, J. S., Rudolph, J. W. & Hatakenaka, S. (2003). Learning from Organizational Experience. In M. Easterby-Smith & M. A. Lyles (eds.), *The Blackwell Handbook of Organizational Learning and Knowledge Management* (pp. 575-600). Malden/USA: Blackwell.

Folke, C., Carpenter, S., Elmqvist, T., Gunderson, L., Holling, C. S. & Walker, B. (2002). Resilience and Sustainable Development: Building Adaptive Capacity in World of Transformations. *Ambio, vol. 31, no. 5*, pp. 437-440.

Hollnagel, E. (2006). Resilience: The Challenge of the Unstable. In E. Hollnagel, D. Woods & N. Leveson (eds.), *Resilience Engineering: Concepts and Precepts*. Burlington: Ashgate.

Hutter, G. (2007). Strategic Planning for Long-Term Flood Risk Management: Some Suggestions for Learning How to Make Strategy at Regional and Local Level. *International Planning Studies, vol. 12, no. 3*, pp. 273-289.

Kuhlicke, C. & Kruse, S. (2009). Nichtwissen und Resilienz in der lokalen Klimaanpassung. Widersprüche zwischen theoriegeleiteten Handlungsempfehlungen und empirischen Befunden am Beispiel des Sommerhochwassers 2002. *GAIA, vol. 18, no. 3*, pp. 247-254.

Mintzberg, H. (1994). *The Rise and Fall of Strategic Planning*. New York: The Free Press.

Müller, B. & Hutter, G. (2009). Dresden als Modellregion zur Klimaanpassung – Das Netzwerkprojekt REGKLAM. *Wissenschaftliche Zeitschrift der TU Dresden, vol. 58, no. 3-4*, pp.112-118.

Overbeck, G., Hartz, A. & Fleischhauer, M. (2008). Ein 10-Punkte-Plan "Klimaanpassung". Raumentwicklungsstrategien zum Klimawandel im Überblick. *Informationen zur Raumentwicklung, no. 6./7.*, pp. 363-380.

Poole, M. S. & Van de Ven, A. H. (1989). Using Paradox to Build Management and Organization Theories. *Academy of Management Review, vol. 14, no. 4*, pp. 562-578.

Schanze, J. (2006). Flood Risk Management – A Basic Framework. In J. Schanze, E. Zeman & J. Marsalek (eds.), *Flood Risk Management: Hazards, Vulnerability and Mitigation Measures* (pp. 1-20). Dordrecht: Springer.

Selle, K. (2005). *Planen. Steuern. Entwickeln. Der Beitrag öffentlicher Akteure zur räumlichen Entwicklung von Stadt und Land*. Dortmund: Rohn.

Sitkin, S. B. (1996). Learning Through Failure: The Strategy of Small Losses. In M. D. Cohen & L. S. Sproull (eds.), *Organizational Learning* (pp. 541-577). Thousand Oaks: Sage.

Sutcliffe, K. & Vogus, T. J. (2003). Organizing for Resilience. In K. S. Cameron, J. E. Dutton & R. E. Quinn (eds.), *Positive Organizational Scholarship. Foundations of a New Discipline* (pp. 94-110). San Francisco: Berrett-Koehler.

Van de Ven, A. H. & Poole, M. S. (1995). Explaining Development and Change in Organizations. *Academy of Management Review, vol. 20, no. 3,* pp. 510-540.

Weick, K. E. & Sutcliffe, K. (2007). *Managing the Unexpected. Resilient Performance in an Age of Uncertainty*. San Francisco: Jossey-Bass.

Wiechmann, T. (2008). *Planung und Adaption. Strategieentwicklung in Regionen, Organisationen und Netzwerken*. Dortmund: Rohn.

Wildavsky, A. (1991). *Searching for Safety*. New Brunswick: Transaction.

Vulnerability and Resilience: A Topic for Spatial Research from a Social Science Perspective

Heiderose Kilper, Torsten Thurmann

1. Introduction

The terms vulnerability and resilience have been the subject of scientific and political discourse for several years. This reflects a growing awareness in the realms of research and politics that potential vulnerabilities and risks must be recognized in a timely manner and that appropriate measures to avoid or contain them must be developed. This task is considered a central challenge of modern 'risk society' (Beck, 1986).

Today, research on aspects of vulnerability and resilience is being conducted in various fields. Sometimes one or both terms are used explicitly, but in other cases the relevant topics are discussed implicitly without using them. For this reason, it is necessary to elucidate the understanding of vulnerability and resilience in each disciplinary context. Due to the complexity and multidimensional nature of vulnerability and resilience, research on the subject doubtless requires interdisciplinary approaches (Tanner, 2006, p. 121). By analogy, dealing with vulnerabilities and developing resilience requires intersectoral political action in terms of a 'governance of preparedness' (Medd & Marvin, 2005).

Linking the terms vulnerability and resilience offers great potential for spatial research from a social science perspective. Research on vulnerability and resilience in a spatial context takes into account the dimensions of risk analysis (vulnerability) as well as sustainability (resilience). In a first step, it separates the dimensions analytically; then it relates them to one another, taking spatial particularities and disparities into consideration.

Against this background, the purpose of this contribution is two-fold: It seeks to present in a heuristic perspective which potential for gaining insights lies in the linked concepts of vulnerability and resilience themselves from a social science point of view. It also seeks to explain in a heuristic perspective which potential for gaining insights can be discerned if the two concepts, vulnerability and resilience, are applied to research questions in social science-based spatial research.

In addition, this contribution aims to present a research project currently under way at the *Leibniz Institute for Regional Development and Structural Planning* (IRS) and scheduled for completion in late 2012. Its goal is to elaborate insights from a social science perspective about:

B. Müller, *German Annual of Spatial Research and Policy 2010*,
German Annual of Spatial Research and Policy,
DOI 10.1007/978-3-642-12785-4_11, © Springer-Verlag Berlin Heidelberg 2011

- The forms, extent, and dynamics of perceived vulnerabilities of subregions,
- The mechanisms of the development of collective awareness of vulnerability in the context of public discourses,
- The triggers, mechanisms, and limited scopes of development of resilience in socio-spatial contexts.

2.   Vulnerability and Resilience as a Pair of Terms

When using the terms vulnerability and resilience, awareness of their ambivalence is of central importance. The terms are used in a variety of ways, depending on the disciplinary context. The concept of resilience originated in ecology (Holling, 1973). Today, however, research on vulnerability and resilience deals with economic, social, and ecological questions, and different focuses can be discerned in each discipline.

Human ecology and research on developing countries have been dealing with questions of vulnerability and resilience for a long time. Human ecology makes human reactions to natural risks and catastrophes such as earthquakes or floods the subject of research. From this perspective, vulnerability is a potential or actual negative impact on social systems and ways of life that is either unforeseeable or cannot be compensated. Accordingly, social resilience is considered successful adaptation on the part of societies to natural risks by avoiding or mitigating damages and disturbances of functions. Research on developing countries, in turn, considers problems of poverty development and the situations of disadvantaged population groups to be the expression of vulnerability due to structural causes. As a result, social vulnerability for individuals and social groups lies in precarious and constantly threatened access to resources necessary for survival, including food, water, and income (Bürkner, 2009).

As of now, other fields in the social sciences are researching aspects of vulnerability and resilience as well. Spatial research (geography including human ecology, spatial planning research, planning sciences) is characterized by a strong thematic focus on natural risks as well as vulnerability and resilience that can be derived from them (Medd & Marvin, 2005). Vulnerability in this context includes the susceptibility of the human-environment system to natural risks and environmental changes such as climate change. Such analyses of vulnerability form the basis for determining adaptation strategies (cf. Stock, Kropp, & Walkenhorst, 2009, p. 98). In the last decade, we have observed a strong research focus in German-speaking countries on current events such as flooding, on the formulation of questions for applied research, and on the elaboration of contextual knowledge to provide orientation for policy and planning (Birkmann, 2008).

In urban research, vulnerability and resilience are topics of research on cities primarily in connection with natural risks (Pelling, 2003) and security, in particular the threats posed by terrorism (Coaffee & Wood, 2006) and crime. The object of research is usually the entire city as the entity under threat. Aspects of vulnerability and resilience are also the focus of research on megacities in developing countries (Kraas & Mertins, 2008).

Social science research on vulnerability and resilience is also conducted in the context of socialization theory and social therapy. Here, the goal is to enable subjects to realize their own vulnerability and to develop resilience. Even if this research relates to individuals, it does yield valuable suggestions for vulnerability and resilience research related to social spaces inasmuch as the two concepts have an action-theoretical orientation. In other words: they are not considered to be 'natural characteristics' but the result of social action, and are viewed in close connection with social relationships.

In spite of the heterogeneity of the terms used in research on vulnerability and resilience, which occasionally results in problems of communication, a common denominator of definitions has been developed which Bürkner (2009, p. 14) summarizes as follows: "'Vulnerability' is considered to be the susceptibility or violability of a person, a social group, or an inanimate object in light of existing hazards, risks, or damaging events which have occurred. As a rule, the violation or damage means that important functions are restricted or no longer existent. 'Resilience' denotes either the ability of individuals, social groups, or objects to compensate for damages which have occurred or to reestablish the functionality that was lost, or the ability to respond flexibly to hazards." This definition of the terms provides the basis for this contribution.

In the works prepared to date, the pair of terms vulnerability and resilience is often characterized by a high degree of normativity. In this contribution, we put forward the opinion that vulnerability is not to be considered negative per se, but certainly also includes opportunities for development. At the same time, resilience does not mean the solution to problems per se; rather, it can also result in unintended effects which in turn can cause problems.

In addition, the aspect of the social differentiation of vulnerability and resilience must be taken into account; that is, not all actors in a particular context are vulnerable to the same degree or able to develop resilience to the same extent. By analogy, this holds true for various sectors as well (cf. Stock et al., 2009, pp. 100).

3. Content-related Focus and Research Questions from the Perspective of Social Science-based Spatial Research

The goal of the research project sketched in the following article is to elaborate insights into relationships between society and space from the perspective of vulnerability and resilience. Without denying the existence of physical space, space is understood as a social construct, i.e., as the result and consequence of human action, which exists for mankind only because of individual and societal ascriptions of meaning. There can be no space beyond the material world, but the perception and evaluation of physical-material structures and the ascription of meaning are always prestructured by society (cf. Löw, 2001). On the basis of this social science conception of space, the definition articulated precisely by Bürkner (2009) is expanded inasmuch as we assume that the vulnerability and resilience of relationships between society and space display higher complexity than can be said of a person, a social group, or an inanimate object. The vulnerability or violability of the relationships between society and space are not understood primarily in the physical-material sense. This would be the case if, for example, the destruction of settlements, built infrastructure, or landscapes by earthquakes, floods, and similar natural risks which can involve injury and loss of human life were of interest, or the existential need of people who live in regions afflicted by drought catastrophes.

The hypothesis upon which the research project is founded is that the vulnerability and resilience of the relationships between society and space exist in a close interrelationship with the way in which certain modes of perception emerge in the public, and how threats that have been identified as such both by science and society are handled institutionally and content-wise (in terms of regulation). For this reason, the public definitions of topics and perceptions of socio-spatial vulnerability and resilience on the one hand and networks, forms of governance, and institutional arrangements as forms of developing resilience on the other are to be examined.

The expectation is that these two content-wise focuses can serve to gain a perspective on the research topic shaped decisively by the social sciences. Dangers are not understood as natural givens. They are considered to be phenomena constructed by society in the sense that certain dangers only become 'realities' by being thematized (publicly) and are only then perceived by members of society. Resilience is not seen to be a technical, static condition, but a societal process that emerges via mechanisms of interaction between actors and the coordination of their actions, and which must be renegotiated time and again as a 'governance of preparedness' (Medd & Marvin, 2005).

In urban and regional development, the formation of networks has been considered the ideal way forward to date: bundling competencies, the assumption goes, can help to solve problems better, different actors working together can enhance the chances that solutions can be implemented. And networks can indeed induce positive effects. But they must not be considered guarantors per se for the development of model solutions and the emergence of resilient structures. For this reason, the task is to elaborate the conditions under which networks, forms of governance, and institutional arrangements are suitable for developing societal potentials for resilience further, and for preventing them from coming to a standstill. The following research questions for empirical study were developed on the basis of these deliberations:

- Which hazards are perceived as vulnerabilities by societal actors and are thematized publicly, and on which spatial and social units are they based?
- Which containment measures are seen as desirable for which hazards to socio-spatial structures?
- In which forms of social organization, in particular in which forms of governance, do processes of mutual understanding, negotiation, and the implementation of relevant measures occur?

- Which institutional provisions to create resilience are developed at which spatial scales, and which concepts of resilience are involved?
- To what extent do cases of the development of resilience result in unintended consequences and occur at the expense of others in certain subregional societies?

The topics which will be addressed in the empirical studies can be allocated to the segments society, economy, and technology/environment.

In the segment society, the topic will be the social vulnerability of spaces, communicated publicly by negative images or dramatizing imputations of problems such as 'emptying', 'becoming desolate', or 'disproportionate ageing of the population'. Measures for developing resilience include interesting approaches to social integration that seek to contribute to improving the quality of life, attractiveness, and also the stigmatized image of urban neighborhoods, cities, and regions, but also initiatives which can be interpreted as regaining the ability of actors to act by overcoming negative self-images as well as negative images in the eyes of others.

In the segment economy, the topic will be individual vulnerabilities and social strategies of forming resilience in the knowledge-based economy. The background for this is the observation that an optimistic tone is currently dominating the discourses about the knowledge-based economy: Knowledge-based activities are considered to offer the most important opportunity, if not the only one, to generate additional, crisis-proof, and well-paid jobs. The circumstance that the knowledge-based economy is also producing new forms of inequality and new forms of precarious employment is a less-prominent part of the discussion. The empirical object of research in this research segment will be the urban labor market for advertising copywriters in Berlin. Thereby, an explicitly metropolitan spatial area of reference has been selected for a segment of the knowledge-based economy in which increased individual vulnerability (hardly institutionalized entry requirements, high fluctuation, difficult career options for older workers) as well as a rich and highly developed palette of social capital strategies to increase resilience should be discernable. In this context, the relationship between small-scale forms of interaction interlinked with an urban milieux, especially face-to-face interaction, and Internet-based networking practices is to be studied.

In the segment technology/environment, the two concepts vulnerability and resilience are to be applied to the topic of natural risks in a specific social science perspective. For the Rhineland region in western Germany, the vulnerability and resilience of water infrastructures and landscapes concerning floods is to be studied from perspectives focusing on the present as on well as historical periods. It is of interest how the vulnerability of this urban technical infrastructure and of cultural landscapes was made a topic of discussion by regional actors in the past, and how it is thematized today, and to which end. Using the example of the problem of low water levels and floods in a small river system in the Brandenburg-Berlin region, the question will be studied as to how the topic of climate change is perceived in the region, and how it is changing the debate about a low water level problem that has existed for decades.

4. Outlook

In the introduction, we formulated the purpose of this contribution as demonstrating which potential for gaining insights for social science-based spatial research lies in the pair of terms vulnerability and resilience. The argument can be summarized as follows.

The concepts of both vulnerability and resilience are considered to be ambivalent. This view relativizes the high degree of normativity often attached to them in the political, but also the scientific debate. It opens the prospects for opportunities for development that lie in risks, be they of an ecological, economic, or social nature, as well as for unintended effects of developments of resilience, which may result in new risks.

By employing theories originating in the social sciences, such as social constructivism as well as concepts of discourses, theories of institutions, and governance concepts, mechanisms of the development of a collective awareness of vulnerability in the context of public discourses can be elaborated on, as well as a new understanding of the social nature of the development of resilience as a 'governance of preparedness' (Medd & Marvin, 2005), and also the dynamics of this process.

The strong thematic focus in vulnerability research on natural risks can be overcome by analyzing negative images of spaces as social and economic hazards as well as precarious work situations as individual hazards in certain sectors of the knowledge-based economy that occur at higher concentrations in particular areas.

The context of these topics, which will be the objects of our empirical research, will provide a new way of studying spatial disparities. What is defined as a hazard, the way in which this occurs, and how public awareness of these hazards is raised or sharpened often differs in various parts of society in different subregions. This also holds true for the actions and processes with which subregional societies desire to respond to the hazards they perceive and which they use as a basis for actively developing measures of resilience. The goal is to elaborate on the relevant differences, to locate them in their specific subregional contexts, and, if possible, to explain them against the background of these subregional constellations of interests.

References

Beck, U. (1986). *Risikogesellschaft. Auf dem Weg in eine andere Moderne.* Frankfurt/M.: Suhrkamp.

Birkmann, J. (2008). Globaler Umweltwandel, Naturgefahren, Vulnerabilität und Katastrophenresilienz. *Raumforschung und Raumordnung, 66(1)*, pp. 5-22.

Bürkner, H.-J. (2009). *Vulnerabilität und Resilienz – Forschungsstand und sozialwissenschaftliche Untersuchungsperspektiven.* Unpublished manuscript.

Coaffee, J. & Wood, D. (2006). The 'Everyday' Resilience of the City. *Human Security and Resilience. ISP/NSC Briefing Paper, 06(1).*

Holling, C. S. (1973). Resilience and Stability of Ecological Systems. *Annual Review of Ecology and Systematics, 4,* pp. 1-23.

Kraas, F. & Mertins, G. (2008). Megastädte in Entwicklungsländern. Vulnerabilität, Informalität, Regier- und Steuerbarkeit. *Geographische Rundschau, 60(11),* pp. 4-10.

Löw, M. (2001). *Raumsoziologie.* Frankfurt/M.: Suhrkamp.

Medd, W. & Marvin, S. (2005). From the Politics of Urgency to the Governance of Preparedness: A Research Agenda on Urban Vulnerability. *Journal of Contingencies and Crisis Management, 13(2),* pp. 44-49.

Pelling, M. (2003). *The Vulnerability of Cities: Social resilience and natural disaster.* London: Earthscan Publications.

Stock, M., Kropp, J. P. & Walkenhorst, O. (2009). Risiken, Vulnerabilität und Anpassungserfordernisse für klimaverletzliche Regionen. *Raumforschung und Raumordnung, 67(2),* pp. 97-113.

Tanner, M. (2006). Risiko, Vulnerabilität und Resilienz. In P. v. Eeuwijk & B. Obrist (eds.), *Vulnerabilität, Migration und Altern: Medizinethnologische Ansätze im Spannungsfeld von Theorie und Praxis* (pp. 119-123). Zürich: Seismo-Verlag.

Adaptability of Regional Planning in Lower Saxony to Climate Change

Enke Franck

1. Climate Change – Dealing with Uncertainty as a Task for Spatial Planning

In this contribution, adaptability is considered to be an aspect of resilience with the goal of dealing successfully with change and shaping it in a sustainable fashion. Using Lower Saxony as an example, this contribution discusses the extent to which the institutional framework of regional planning appears to be suitable for confronting the challenges of climate change.

Most of the expected effects of climate change display spatial aspects and consequences. Accordingly, adaptive measures must be employed in a spatial context. Weighing decisions between different land uses and preparing long-term programs and plans are among the classic tasks of spatial planning. In this vein, the federal government assigned spatial planning, as an integrative cross-sectoral task, a pioneering role in the development of guiding principles for adaptable and resilient spatial structures in the 'German Strategy for Adaptation to Climate Change'. The EU's White Paper: 'Adapting to Climate Change', published in 2009, also emphasizes the necessity of a strategic spatial planning concept with a long-term approach. At the regional level, however, this has been realized only in rudimentary form to date. More recent studies (e.g., Overbeck, Sommerfeldt, Köhler, & Birkmann, 2009, pp. 193-203) on the way German regional planning handles climate change demonstrate that although the topic of preventive climate protection has been taken up in most of the regional spatial planning programs in Lower Saxony, they include few direct statements concerning adaptation to climate change. Even though the regional planners themselves expect that competition between the various land uses will intensify due to climate change in the future.

A central problem when considering regional planning and climate change is dealing with uncertainty. Although climate modeling has made great progress in recent years, its results are still projections which cannot be exact, not least because of the uncertainty regarding future socio-economic development alone (Walkenhorst & Stock, 2009). But what we know about climate change even today must be used to adapt actions and develop robust planning strategies. Accordingly, spatial development plans should be flexible, not only to be able to respond to possible deviations from the climate prognoses: we must also 'expect the unexpected' and include radical surprises in plans. These demands cause a dilemma, as the reliable

B. Müller, *German Annual of Spatial Research and Policy 2010*,
German Annual of Spatial Research and Policy,
DOI 10.1007/978-3-642-12785-4_12, © Springer-Verlag Berlin Heidelberg 2011

and firm formulations of goals and the conventional printed maps of the regional spatial planning programs appear to contradict the demanded procedural and resilient strategies of adaptation to climate change.

2. Adapting to Climate Change – Possibilities and Limitations of Regional Planning in Lower Saxony

In line with current assessments of regional climate development (an increase in the average temperature, damper winters, and more severe summer droughts are to be expected in Lower Saxony) and the various scenarios for sea-level rise, the focus of planning efforts will be on the topics of flood protection and coastal protection as well as the changes in agriculture and forestry, most of which are also linked to water. Therefore, water management will play a fundamental role in Lower Saxony.

One special feature of Lower Saxony's planning is that in principle (with the exception of 'Greater Braunschweig' and the 'Hanover Region'), the counties are responsible for regional planning. The advantage of this locally-based system is that the planning regions are manageable in size and that regional specifics – such as regional climate changes and special regional vulnerabilities – can be taken into consideration directly in regional spatial planning programs. As recent changes in the state spatial planning law of Lower Saxony as well as in state planning have for the most part permitted regional authorities to develop instruments and plan symbols, it is possible to achieve customized regional solutions. However, in many counties, regional planning suffers from a lack of acceptance even in municipal politics. Simply toughening the existing instruments in a regionally adapted way would therefore probably face widespread political resistance. All the more as there have been efforts for years to pare down spatial development plans, and climate adaptation is now a new topic which could be linked to instruments in the regional plan being sharpened or even newly implemented.

One disadvantage of regional planning being at the local level lies in the often very restricted resources in terms of personnel and finances (even 'one-person agencies') that often reach the limits of their capacity during major planning procedures and extensive innovations. These limited capacities of individual regional planners in turn support cooperation, which is to be welcomed, as well as an exchange of experiences among planners in neighboring areas or those affected by similar issues. New and exemplary structures of cooperation in regional and state planning include the *Forum for Urban and Regional Planning in the Extended Economic Area Hanover* and the *Spatial Structure Working Group* of the metropolitan region Bremen-Oldenburg offer planners a framework for jointly supported ideas and projects in addition to opportunities for exchange.

The lack of horizontal integration between public authorities in Germany must be considered an obstacle to an interdisciplinary approach and integrated treatment of climate change on the part of regional planning. Spatial development plans are prepared on the basis of sectoral plans and then decided upon in the political process. This is why the agencies responsible for strong sectoral plans are capable of blocking spatial development plans if they feel they have not been taken into account adequately. Good solutions can be expected in win-win situations, on the other hand, when a sectoral plan hopes to gain advantages by being implemented in the regional spatial development programs, e.g., landscape master planning vying to achieve a more strongly binding status. The situation is similar for Lower Saxony regional planning when cooperating with municipalities belonging to counties which naturally have a strong influence where municipalities are responsible for spatial planning. Direct negotiations are often required to reach agreement on provisions and goals of regional spatial development programs. But in the case of climate adaptation in particular, it is essential for municipalities to be on board; after all, adaptation and implementation must also take place at the local level.

In the same vein, regional planning aims to guide future land use, but it has no means to influence existing land use or the extant building stock. It is the building stock, however, that has the largest amount of damage potential, that is affected by climate-induced extreme events (such as flooding), and that would actually have to adapt to changing climate conditions. Here there is a lack of political will to implement measures – spatial planning goals are not applied to the existing situation (of settlements and other land uses) for fear of claims for compensation.

3. Adapting to Climate Change – The Necessity of Integrated Approaches

Regional planning has no binding effect on agriculture or forestry, either; despite them representing the two largest land uses in the federal state of Lower Saxony, which has a strong agricultural character. Competing land use claims will become more common, in particular concerning climate change. For example, production of biomass may conflict with conventional agriculture with its focus on food and feedstuff production, and it can also endanger biological diversity. Presumably, guiding land uses by means of spatial planning will succeed only if linked with agricultural aid. Initial approaches in this direction include, for example, the 'Integrated Rural Development Concepts' (ILEKS) prepared by the *Lower Saxony Ministry for Food, Agriculture, Consumer Protection and Regional Development*, which is also responsible for state spatial planning. State development and state planning could and should be interwoven more closely here.

This discussion shows that the localized planning system in Lower Saxony has advantages and disadvantages. With regard to the growing demands for coordination and the increasing importance of cooperation and communication in climate adaptation, the question arises as to the system's effectiveness in light of limited resources. How flexible and adaptable is Lower Saxony regional planning itself in dealing with climate change? Which approaches should be developed further, which obstacles should be removed? Which underlying conditions are necessary for integrated approaches?

The questions mentioned here form a core theme of the five-year cross-cutting project IMPLAN (Implementation of Results from KLIFF in Spatial Planning in Lower Saxony), which began in early 2009 as part of the Lower Saxony joint research project KLIFF (Climate Impact Research) – Scenarios for Climate Adaptation. In close cooperation with regional and state planning, ways and means of adapting to climate change are to be demonstrated.

For more information see: www.kliff-niedersachsen.de

References

Overbeck, G., Sommerfeldt, P., Köhler, S. & Birkmann, J. (2009). Klimawandel und Regionalplanung. *Raumforschung und Raumordnung, 67(2),* pp. 193-203.

Walkenhorst, O. & Stock, M. (2009). Regionale Klimaszenarien für Deutschland. Eine Leseanleitung. *E-Papers of the ARL, no. 6.*

Dealing with Climate Change – The Opportunities and Conflicts of Integrating Mitigation and Adaptation

Sebastian Ebert

1. Introduction

There are frequent calls to integrate strategies for climate mitigation and adaptation regarding the unavoidable consequences of climate change. Taking an integrated view appears reasonable especially in planning practice; after all, we now have a broad range of experience concerning climate mitigation, in contrast to climate adaptation. This is shown, for example, by the results of a written survey carried out among regional planning agencies in Germany in 2008 by the 'Climate Change and Spatial PlanningWorking Group' of the *Academy for Spatial Research and Planning* (ARL). At the European level, the situation in the Baltic Sea Region is comparable. The *Centre for Climate Science and Policy Research* (CSPR/Linköping University, Sweden) carried out a written survey in 2009 among six Target Areas in Germany, Sweden, Finland, Estonia, Latvia, and Lithuania within the framework of the EU project 'BalticClimate', which is headed by the ARL. Here, too, knowledge about climate mitigation was stronger than that about adaptation to the consequences of climate change. An integrated perspective seems to be required: neither a thematic shift from mitigation to the relatively new policy of adaptation is desired, nor are authorities meant to choose between both. In the following paper, the question is of interest as to which aspects of climate mitigation can also be employed as starting points for adaptation strategies. The opportunities and conflicts of integration in guiding spatial development processes will be sketched out briefly, using some examples.

In general, climate mitigation in Germany has already found its place at the levels of regional and local planning. Provisions on the expansion of renewable energy and the development of low-emission and energy efficient settlement patterns are given priority. An indirect climate protection effect is also linked to protecting undeveloped open spaces which have the function of carbon sinks (especially forest and marshland). Since 2008, the focus of attention has increasingly shifted to adaptation to the consequences of climate change, supported not least by the 'German Adaptation Strategy'. The task of spatial planning is to tackle additional effects of extreme weather events above and beyond the previously recognized area of precautionary flood control, but also impacts of incremental changes in the long run. They are the result of the projections for Germany: a temperature increase in the summer, accompanied by decreasing amounts of precipitation, as well as milder winters with increasing precipitation.

B. Müller, *German Annual of Spatial Research and Policy 2010*,
German Annual of Spatial Research and Policy,
DOI 10.1007/978-3-642-12785-4_13, © Springer-Verlag Berlin Heidelberg 2011

2. Examples of Synergies and Conflicts

The expansion of renewable energy sources, central to climate protection, is associated with a diversification of energy generation and simultaneously results in a decentralization of supply infrastructures. The consumers of energy produced from renewable sources – hydropower, biomass, wind power, solar thermal energy, photovoltaics, and geothermics – are in many cases located closer to the specific place of production. Conventional forms of energy production, most of which damage the climate, are linked to more highly centralized infrastructures. The expansion of renewable energy provides a good opportunity to achieve synergies in adapting to the consequences of climate change. In this context, it is of strategic importance that both diversified energy production and decentralized structures display lower vulnerability to extreme weather events. Spatial planning can and should contribute to ensuring greater security of supply by securing spaces for renewable energy production as well as the supply infrastructure adapted to it. Regional energy concepts could prove to be useful instruments for integrating climate mitigation and adaptation. Of the various forms of renewable energy, wind power, biomass (energy crops), and open space photovoltaic installations are more suitable for rural areas due to their extensive land requirements. Nonetheless, especially solar thermal energy/photovoltaics are also options for high-density areas. When considering strategies for expanding renewable energies, in particular in rural areas, the question arises as to what extent they can have positive effects for regional value added besides synergies for climate adaptation.

Spatial planning research has identified initial lines of conflict between climate mitigation and adaptation when it comes to the development of settlement patterns. For example, they are to be developed to form compact urban bodies following the guiding principle of inner urban development where the distances to be covered are short and motorized traffic plays a minor role, thereby permitting the entire transport sector to be organized to achieve low emissions. The goal of reducing transportation-induced greenhouse gases by means of an approach based on settlement patterns can, however, also be considered counterproductive for the intensity of climate impacts. The probability that compact cities with insufficient fresh air conduits connecting them to the surrounding areas become urban heat islands increases. This impact on the microclimate is intensified additionally by global climate change. Therefore, we must discuss the question of how the guiding principle of inner urban development can combine urban density optimized in terms of transportation with the open spaces necessary in terms of the climate. This in turn is linked to the question as to an additional contribution to global climate mitigation: To what extent, for example, should open spaces within the urban fabric be developed into nearly natural areas for renewable energies (the cultivation of energy crops on short-rotation plantations)? Can this make a substantial contribution to climate mitigation, or are the areas needed for other uses such as recreation? Such deliberations about climate mitigation and adaptation are relevant in particular in processes of urban and regional shrinking that are associated with lowering densities and often reach limits for increasing transportation efficiency.

Protecting undeveloped open spaces (priority areas or reserve areas) with their indirect significance for climate mitigation is a non-negligible task. Although spatial planning focuses on forests and marshland, for instance, in terms of their importance for nature protection, they can also serve as carbon sinks. In addition, some of these areas can be suitable as retention areas for precautionary flood control. The concepts for adapting to the danger of rising river water levels increasingly include packages of measures above and beyond building up the height of dikes. Securing additional retention areas for floodwaters is becoming more important. Spatial planning can employ the instruments of priority areas or reserve areas for this purpose as well. Synergy effects between flood control, nature protection, and climate mitigation (by strengthening the function of carbon sinks) are possible in some types of natural areas, but they also require land uses that are adapted accordingly. Intensive land use, by contrast, can have negative effects on the climate and biodiversity. Therefore, additional actors besides spatial planning must contribute to the development and implementation of strategies.

3. Conclusions

The examples outlined demonstrate that in both rural and urban areas, different aspects of climate mitigation can also be employed as starting points for adaptation to climate impacts; however, conflicts between the two fields may arise as well. The specifics of climate mitigation and adaptation also justify additional analysis that is independent of each other. Detecting all synergies between all relevant issues would not be realistic despite strong efforts. But at least climate mitigation strategies and measures should not reduce adaptive capacity, and adaptation strategies and measures should not run counter to the goal of climate mitigation. In addition, policy options of dealing with climate change should not be developed without taking further major challenging factors such as demographic and economic changes into consideration, so that additional potentials or conflicts can be identified. Spatial planning in Germany is characterized by weighing many interests, which amounts to a special competence for comprehensive strategic integration. How this can succeed in the Baltic countries is to be elucidated in the EU project 'BalticClimate'.

Regional Climate Adaptation Research – The Implementation of an Integrative Regional Approach in the Dresden Model Region

Alfred Olfert, Jana Planek

1. The Necessity of Regional Climate Adaptation Research

Global climate change is one of the greatest challenges of our time (IPCC, 2007). Particularly industrial countries are heavily dependent on continuously functioning structures that serve as the basis for future development and prosperity (Stern, 2006). These structures are often vulnerable to meteorological hazards such as heat, extreme precipitation, and flooding. Adapting to the inevitable consequences of climate change is therefore a central task of modern-day society.

Approaches to climate change adaptation and climate protection are fundamentally different. Climate protection addresses globally identical drivers of climate change and is therefore based on similar measures around the world. The impacts of climate change vary according to region and are dependent on existing natural, economic, and social parameters. These differences require specially tailored adaptation measures for each potentially affected issue even though a general set of options for adaptation may exist.

A first step towards adaptation is to gain and to communicate a detailed understanding of the extent of the regional shift in climatic and atmospheric parameters and the socio-economic reactions linked to them. The resulting effects on society call for a holistic cross-sectoral consideration of both the risks posed by climate change as well as the prospects for the region in question (Bundesregierung, 2009).

With this in mind, strategies for dealing with the regional effects of climate change as a complementary component to climate change are gaining in importance. The *German Federal Ministry of Education and Research* has strengthened regional adaptation research with its program 'KLIMZUG – Climate Change in Future Oriented Regions'. Throughout Germany seven model regions have been awarded network-oriented research projects dealing with specific issues of adaptation to climate change. One such project is entitled the Development and Testing of an 'Integrated Regional Climate Adaptation Program for the Dresden Model Region' (REGKLAM).

B. Müller, *German Annual of Spatial Research and Policy 2010*,
German Annual of Spatial Research and Policy,
DOI 10.1007/978-3-642-12785-4_14, © Springer-Verlag Berlin Heidelberg 2011

2. REGKLAM – An Integrated Regional Project Concerning Adaptation to Climate Change

The REGKLAM Region describes an area defined by existing administrative boundaries and established economic links (Fig. 1). It includes the area of the Regional Planning Association along the upper Elbe Valley, as well as economically strongly related areas around Freiberg to the west and western Lusatia (up to Bautzen) to the east. This is a concept based on the ongoing discussion of the so-called 'Dresden Economic Region'.

Fig. 1: REGKLAM – Dresden Model Region. Source: REGKLAM (2009).

The guiding principle for work in the REGKLAM project is to ensure the quality of life while taking advantage of economic opportunities in order to increase the future competitiveness of the region. This principle adheres to the stipulation made in the KLIMZUG program. Within this context REGKLAM has formulated three main objectives that should make a long-term contribution to the region's future prospects:

(a) The development of an implementation-oriented 'Integrated Regional Climate Adaptation Program' (IRKAP),
(b) The initiation and support of key projects and additional adaptation measures,
(c) The consolidation of a regional network of actors.

Project work in REGKLAM is divided into three main modules. Each module consists of several subprojects which have specific thematic areas of focus (Fig. 2). A fourth module deals with scientific project management and coordination (Module 4).

The main product of the REGKLAM project is the 'Integrated Regional Climate Adaptation Program' (IRKAP), developed within Module 1. On the one hand, the IRKAP's purpose is to summarize projections of future development, adaptation measures, and other results achieved in the project in a form easily understandable to decision makers and other actors. On the other hand, however, the IRKAP serves as an instrument designed to support the implementation of adaptation measures and it will be agreed upon by key regional actors involved in the project (Objective 1). Module 3 develops climate change adaptation measures for REGKLAM's three priority topics: settlement patterns, water systems, and land use. The main objective here is to secure and increase the economic potential of the region by providing innovation. The range of intended adaptation measures will be accompanied by instruments that shape the framework of action, e.g., amendments to rules and guidelines or the realignment of funding programs. It is intended that the implementation of individual measures be initiated in the course of the project (Objective 2).

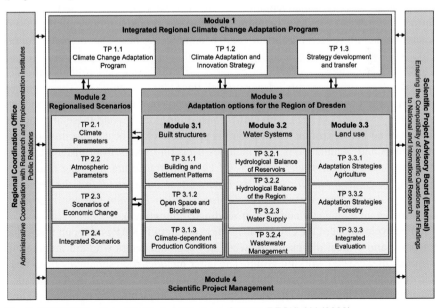

Fig. 2: REGKLAM – Scientific Project Structure. Source: REGKLAM (2008).

A common basis for the development of adaptation measures for the Dresden Region is ensured by providing project-wide accepted projections of climatic and socio-economic change and through the application of similar time slices. Climatic and atmospheric changes are considered by referring to the 'Intergovernmental Panel on Climate Change' (IPCC) scenarios A1b, A2, and B1. Adaptation measures are developed for three time slices in response to the different planning horizons actors have: (a) 1991 until today, describing current changes for the short term planning horizon, (b) 2021-2050 for the mid-term planning horizon, (c) 2071-2100 with respect to the long-term planning horizon.

The success of efforts both to develop an implementation-oriented program and to actually implement what is needed to adapt largely depends on the early, close, and sustained cooperation of key actors from scientific, political, administrative, and economic sectors. An explicit objective of the project is therefore also the establishment and consolidation of an interest-based network of actors who are able to co-operate for the duration of the project and beyond (Objective 3). Consistent to the approach of the KLIMZUG program, REGKLAM is pursuing a regional approach in the areas of climate impact research and adaptation research. With regard to adaptation research, the regional approach places a great deal of importance on the integration of content, approach, and actors, as opposed to the sectoral approach, which has a strong emphasis on specific themes.

3.   REGKLAM – Work in a Regional Network

In order to support implementation of the project's results, REGKLAM was formed from the outset as a network of numerous regional representatives from scientific, administrative, political, and economic sectors. The project's initial proposal was submitted by seven partners: the *Leibniz Institute of Ecological and Regional Development* (coordination), the *TU Dresden* (ten departments), the *TU Bergakademie Freiberg* (three departments), the *Leibniz Institute for Tropospheric Research,* the *City of Dresden*, the *Dresden Groundwater Research Centre*, and the *Stadtentwässerung Dresden*. The entire consortium goes beyond these and ranges from state authorities (often with a scientific perspective), to local authorities, private companies and organizations, and includes decision-makers from different levels of public administration and politics. Of key importance are the state ministries involved (e.g., the *State Ministry of the Environment and Agriculture*), the *Regional Planning Association*, and the *Stadt-Umland-Region Dresden* (an administrative network set up by the city and its surrounding communities).

The development of the climate adaptation program IRKAP is an open forum for intensive and critical discussion between key regional actors who are involved in a specifically created working group. The latter includes representatives from state and regional planning departments, two state ministries, as well as the Dresden Chamber of Commerce. The development and implementation of adaptation measures is also supported by an economic advisory board that consists of reference companies from a variety of branches. It will give the REGKLAM findings a critical examination from an economic point of view and will also make recommendations. Additionally, the so-called political talks will focus the options to sensitively handle climate change in the political arena. The timely involvement of the political sector will help identify the most promising point of time and the ideal mode of communication for ensuring the appropriate implementation of project findings.

References

Bernhofer, C., Matschullat, J. & Bobeth, A. (eds.) (2009). *Das Klima in der REGKLAM Modellregion Dresden*. Berlin: Rhombos Verlag.

Bundesregierung (ed.) (2009). *Deutsche Anpassungsstrategie an den Klimawandel*. Berlin.

IPCC – Intergovernmental Panel on Climate Change (2007). Climate Change 2007: The Physical Science Basis. Contribution of Working Group I to the Fourth Assessment, Report of the Intergovernmental Panel on Climate Change. In S. Solomon, D. Qin, M. Manning, Z. Chen, M. Marquis, K. B. Averyt, M. Tignor & H. L. Miller (eds.), Cambridge (UK/USA): Cambridge University Press.

Müller, B. & Hutter, G. (2009). Dresden als Modellregion zur Klimaanpassung – Das Netzwerkprojekt REGKLAM. *Wissenschaftliche Zeitschrift der TU Dresden, Vol. 58, No. 3-4*, pp.112-118.

Nicholas Stern (2006). *The Stern Review of the Economics of Climate*. London: Cabinet Office – HM Treasury.

River Landscapes – Reference Areas for Regionally Specific Adaptation Strategies to Climate Change

Andreas Vetter, Frank Sondershaus

1.   Introduction

The development of river landscapes poses a particular challenge in the course of climate change. A shifting of annual precipitation from the summer to the winter season and increasing frequencies of extreme events (drought, heavy precipitation) are forecast for central Europe. Triggered by the dramatic flooding events in Germany in recent years (1997, 2002), government action is increasingly focusing on flood prevention as well as on the prevention of extreme low water levels. The research project 'Linking precautionary flood protection to the development of regional cultural landscapes in river landscapes: An analysis taking into account the effects of climate change on low water levels', commissioned by the *Federal Office for Building and Regional Planning*, was conceived against this background. Building upon analyses of the literature and of institutions, researchers identified existing overlaps of the fields of action studied as well as potential synergies and conflicts of interest. Best practice approaches were profiled in additional case studies, and strategic recommendations, especially for water management and spatial planning, were formulated. The main results of this study are presented below.

2.   Linking Precautionary Flood Protection and Preventing Low Water Levels with the Development of Regional Cultural Landscapes

In contrast to traditional, largely technical flood protection, the contemporary approach to precautionary flood control is based on a broadened perspective that includes, for example, the appropiate planning of settlements or the renaturation of flood plains. This development has made flood control more complex and has increased its relevance for cultural landscapes. Parallel to this process, the development of regional cultural landscapes is establishing itself as a policy field. It has developed from a sectoral, protective approach focusing on individual characteristics of the cultural landscape (e.g., historic elements) into a cross-sectoral concept of sustainable regional development encompassing the entire area in question and including all activities that leave their mark on the landscape. In

B. Müller, *German Annual of Spatial Research and Policy 2010*,
German Annual of Spatial Research and Policy,
DOI 10.1007/978-3-642-12785-4_15, © Springer-Verlag Berlin Heidelberg 2011

doing so, the fields of action mentioned above are converging in a process with respect to three dimensions: expanded 'spatial scope', increasing 'complexity' of the approaches and the space they refer to, and effects on 'identity'. This convergence can also be applied to precaution for low water levels. The existing overlaps provide for synergies if the policy fields are viewed jointly, but they can also result in potential conflicts of interests.

These reciprocal relationships between the development of regional cultural landscapes and precautionary flood protection on the one hand and preventing low water levels on the other were examined in the relevant laws and documents at the European, federal, and state level. In summary, it can be stated that the formal documents relating to precautionary flood protection do not mention existing overlaps with the development of regional cultural landscapes as such. The existing relationships, however, provide a foundation for an institutional linking of the policy fields. One example is the demand to 'give rivers more space' in the federal government's '5 Point Program for the Improvement of Preventive Flood Control Measures' (BMVBS, 2002). Due to the informal nature of promoting regional cultural landscapes, there are only informal overlaps with flood protection and preventing low water levels to date. At the federal level (for example, in spatial planning), the 'Concepts and Strategies for Spatial Development in Germany' strengthen an interlinked view (Concept 3: Conservation of resources; shaping of cultural landscapes). Conflicts between different goals are not readily apparent from the documents alone, but they can be identified in particular at the levels of goals and measures of concrete projects. For example, developing areas close to river banks may compete with keeping them free of development in order to serve as flooding areas. As hardly any formal regulations exist to date regarding precautions for low water levels, the relevant documents do not include any linkage to the development of regional cultural landscapes. Existing synergies and possible contradictions can, however, be derived from informal documents, so it will indeed be possible to take them into account if and when this field of action is institutionalized in the future.

3.   Experiences from Regional Case Studies in Germany

To complement the analyses of documents, the interlinkages of the policy fields with the approaches for dealing with climate change at the regional level mentioned above were examined in case studies. Urban and rural cultural landscapes in the upper and lower reaches of rivers were incorporated in the study in order to consider the various perspectives and situations of the dynamics of flooding and low water levels. These criteria were employed to select four regions as case studies: 'Havel Region' (Brandenburg), 'Fränkisches Seenland' (Bavaria), 'Emscher Region', and 'Regionale 2010' (both in North Rhine-Westphalia). The two latter case studies in urban-suburban river landscapes will be described in more detail here.

The Emscher Region is an urban region in the Ruhr Area with a high degree of impermeable surface area. Local heavy precipitation events have a strong effect on flooding dynamics, and possibilities for setting aside land to mitigate such effects are limited. In order to deal with the uncertainties regarding the impacts of climate change on flooding and low water levels, the water board (Emschergenossenschaft) is pursuing a no-regret strategy, in other words, it is carrying out measures that will have positive effects regardless of the projections. One example of such measures is on-site rainwater infiltration. The *Emschergenossenschaft* is not the only institution to orient its water management activities toward the entire catchment area of the Emscher. The *Regionalverband Ruhr* does, as well, and is a key actor relevant for the cultural landscape. Master plans conceived to link the two fields of action have been prepared. Therefore, long-term visions exist for rebuilding the river landscape in terms of water management (Masterplan Emscher Zukunft) and for the integrated development of the cultural landscape (Masterplan Emscher Landschaftspark 2010). Regional actors in the Emscher Region consider the development of river landscapes to be an important foundation for the ecological and economic reconstruction of an old industrialized region.

The project area of the 'Regionale 2010' is characterized by the Rhine as well as the cities of Cologne, Bonn, and Leverkusen, which are located along its banks. The region is strongly affected by flooding and is highly dependent on activities upstream on the Rhine. The 'Regionale 2010' is an instrument of structural policy of the state of North Rhine-Westphalia, and it includes perspectives for the river landscape pertaining to regional economics as well as culture. The 'Regionale 2010' bundles projects regarding integrated cultural landscape development, some of which also take concerns of precautionary flood protection into account. However, the projects often display ambivalence between focusing on the river and the necessity of securing areas for controlled flooding. The 'masterplan :grün' developed within the framework of the 'Regionale 2010' serves as an informal coordinating instrument for developing the river landscape. Valuable areas of the cultural landscapes are identified in the 'masterplan :grün', and the floodplain corridors are elaborated as 'blue ribbons' that are pivotal areas of economic und cultural development. The master plan is also to take up the topic of climate change when it is developed further in the future. The 'Regionale 2010' is an integrated and communicative approach to developing the river landscape in a manner referring to the cultural landscape; the approach intentionally takes up the identity-producing function of the Rhine and supports enhancing the river's value to the region.

The selected case studies make clear that at the project level, the added value of linking the development of regional cultural landscapes with precautions against flooding and low water levels in river landscapes has already been recognized and partially realized in individual cases. The cooperation required for this was put into practice by using specific instruments (intermunicipal associations, master plans, cross-sectoral studies, networks, etc.) whose spatial focus is oriented to the river landscape. Awareness of the problem of climate change exists in principle; however, the uncertainties of the projections are a great challenge to planning and will continue to be in the long term. The problem of low water levels, which will become more severe as climate change progresses, is recognized as a field of action by the various actors, but no comprehensive low water level management exists. The role of regional planning has so far been limited to its legally mandated core function of land use planning for flood protection.

4. Climate Change as a Long-term Challenge for Spatial Planning and Water Management – Recommendations

The term 'river landscape' should be used as a strategic concept to link the perspectives of precaution against flooding and low water levels as well as the development of regional cultural landscapes to one another, thereby doing justice to the increased demands in dealing with these fields of action. From an actor-based perspective, the river landscape is also an area of action for implementing additional, multi-functional goals such as economic development, recreational use, and water-based tourism. Against the background of problems whose severity is intensifying due to climate change, river landscapes should be considered focal areas of regionally specific climate adaptation strategies. This is not a sectoral, technical task, but rather a joint regional task which involves water management and spatial planning in major roles.

For this reason, it is recommended that spatial planning integrate river landscapes as reference areas for dealing with the demands of climate change into strategies for climate adaptation. Regional planning should take extreme events into account in the context of a forward-looking allocation of space, as such events are expected to become more common in the future. Demands for space as well as the different vulnerabilities of various land uses, which are influenced by factors related to the built environment, ecosystems, social determinants, and institutions, are to be considered in regional plans. Water management should develop flexible adaptation strategies to meet the requirements posed by the uncertainties of climate projections. No-regret strategies, for example, are suitable for this purpose. In addition, it may be necessary to reexamine and reassess water management and transportation plans and decisions of the past against the background of climate change ('climate proofing').

Pilot projects should be initiated to test innovative approaches and to generate additional ideas and experiences in dealing with the challenges mentioned above – with a view to increasing the resilience of river landscapes facing the impacts of climate change. The focus on particularly vulnerable river landscapes is intended to deepen experience with handling uncertainties, as they have all too often resulted in a 'wait-and-see' attitude. In addition, integrated and sustainable river landscape development poses a multitude of conceptional requirements: participation and strategic communication are to be implemented systematically, and spatial integration requirements as well as the various political and administrative levels are to be taken into account at all times. The project publication contains recommendations for handling these challenges.

References

BMVBS (Bundesministerum für Verkehr, Bau und Stadtentwicklung) (ed.) (2002). *5-Punkte-Programm der Bundesregierung. Arbeitsschritte zur Verbesserung des vorbeugenden Hochwasserschutzes.* Berlin. Retrieved from: http://www.bmvbs.de/Anlage/original_925224/Fuenf-Punkte-Programm-der-Bundesregierung-zum-vorbeugenden-Hochwasserschutz_-2002.pdf

Link to the project publication: www.bbsr.bund.de
Flusslandschaften – Wechselbeziehungen zwischen regionaler Kulturlandschafts-gestaltung, vorbeugendem Hochwasserschutz und Niedrigwasservorsorge
(Werkstatt: Praxis, Heft 67).

Strategic Planning – Approaches to Coping with the Crisis of Shrinking Cities

Manfred Kühn, Susen Fischer

1. The Crisis of Shrinking Cites in Eastern Germany

In eastern Germany the overwhelming majority of cities, especially the medium-sized ones, have been faced with the crisis of shrinkage since the 1990s. Shrinking cities are characterized by the multi-dimensional interaction of different challenges: Demographic problems have been caused by a decline in population due to a lack of births, migration, and the aging of residents. Urban economic problems involve the loss of employment due to de-industrialization. Because job losses linked to de-industrialization could not be compensated for by growth within the service sector, shrinkage has been especially prevalent in older industrial cities. Urban problems include an overcapacity of public infrastructure, large brownfield areas, and vacant residential and commercial property. These demographic and socio-economic processes of decline have resulted in weakened financial conditions within the affected municipalities, which have in turn greatly limited local government's scope of action.

2. Wanted: Strategies for Coping with Structural Change

And thus urban politicians and planners are faced with the large task of simultaneously solving demographic, economic, and urban structural change within shrinking cities. In older industrial cities the creation of resilience is particularly important, and requires a thorough redefinition of the cities' identities and a specific profiling so that they can compete with other communities as suitable locations for business. In order to regenerate shrinking cities, integrated strategies have been demanded once again, even though suitable models of these have not yet been tested. In western European planning sciences the 'managing of spatial change' has been specifically defined as a strategic urban planning task for several decades. In de-industrialized cities such as Manchester, Bilbao, and Barcelona strategic concepts, visions, and projects have been developed. But to what degree can these approaches be transferred to medium-sized cities in eastern Germany? And what basic conditions are necessary in order to actually use and implement these strategic planning approaches in de-industrialized cities, and which factors may actually impede the use of strategic planning in these communities?

B. Müller, *German Annual of Spatial Research and Policy 2010*,
German Annual of Spatial Research and Policy,
DOI 10.1007/978-3-642-12785-4_16, © Springer-Verlag Berlin Heidelberg 2011

We investigated these questions within the framework of a project financed by the *Deutsche Forschungsgemeinschaft* (the DFG is Germany's central self-governing research funding organization) entitled 'Strategic Urban Planning. Approaches to the Regeneration of Shrinking Cities in Eastern Germany'. To this end, a normative model was developed that defines 'Strategic Urban Planning' as the revolving interaction between strategic visions (as long-term general frameworks of orientation for urban development) and strategic projects (as short-term area-based steps of implementation in specific local governance constellations). Empirical case studies were also carried out in the cities of Cottbus, Dessau, Görlitz, Stralsund, and Wittenberge.

3. Empirical Results in Five Medium-sized Eastern German Cities

The following selected results of the case studies are particularly relevant with regard to the main elements of the model of strategic urban planning (visions, projects, cooperation among the actors involved). For a complete description of the investigation and the results please see: Kühn and Fischer (2010).

3.1 Long-term and City-wide Visions of Development

Case studies show that visioning processes are necessary elements of communal strategy formulation, but that vision results are often insufficient with regard to giving cities a new image. Only a small percentage of the visions found in cities fulfilled all of the requirements defined in a model of strategic development: interdepartmental development under the leadership of the mayor, public participation processes between the political, administrative, economic, and civil society sectors, political consensus ('shared future'), and image-building. In the practice of urban development policies, visions are often caught between differing demands and dilemmas due to the individual logic of the actors involved.

Political leadership versus participation

If visions are to gain strategic importance in the sense of the model, they require a broadly public process of negotiation that is open to stimuli from civil society. These types of visions have a stronger local political orientational function than those which are developed top-down by political leaders. In cities without visioning processes, conflicts between different groups of actors concerning the overall strategic orientation will be greater and more common than in cities in which a consensus about the long-term orientation of urban development has been worked out in a public process of negotiation.

Specialization versus diversification

Broadly negotiated visioning processes usually have more diversified results. Often, however, actors expect that a sharper profile of the city will be gained during a development model process, ranging from an identification of the city's special strengths to unique features the city has in comparison with other urban areas. While diversification may lead to a danger of arbitrariness, a strong specialization may include the risk of one-sided monostructures. Visioning processes in cities are not powerful enough to manage conflicts between different public and private actors or to moderate them. Existing pressure in cities to reach a political consensus often leads to compromise solutions. The results of visioning processes then reveal the coexistence of different and sometimes conflicting orientations. The price of this may be an overall lack of general, long-term orientation for actors.

Cognitive self-images versus marketable external images

Strategic visions address both those within a city as well as those on the outside. In terms of marketing considerations, visions are coupled to expectations that a new image of the city will be created, which can then be communicated externally. Externally, visions have the function of improving the often negative image cities have for non-local firms, the media, and tourists due to their industrial heritage (e.g., Cottbus as a 'grimy' city located within the former East German brown coal region). As far as many actors are concerned, however, the more important function strategic visions have lies in the political process of understanding with regard to cognitive self-images. Visions therefore have the internal function of creating a local consensus (based on social participatory and negotiating processes) between actors from politics, administration, and civil society regarding a community's self-image, and to provide long-term orientation for urban development. This local political consensus is stronger in some cases (e.g., Stralsund) and weaker (e.g., Dessau) in others.

3.2 Short-term and Area-based Projects

In medium-sized cities three different types of projects have been set up: infrastructure projects, events, and urban cultural projects. Cultural projects are being assigned a key role in the regeneration of the cities involved. These will either occur in cities in the form of temporary events (e.g., the 'Elbland Festival' in Wittenberge) or symbolic architectural structures (e.g., the 'Ozeaneum' in Stralsund and the 'Kulturbrücke' in Görlitz). It is expected that these cultural projects will help transform the images of the cities involved and provide an impetus for cultural tourism. Following the example of the 'Guggenheim Museum' in Bilbao, actors are hoping for the 'Bilbao Effect'. Temporary projects such as the 'BUGA 1995' (National Garden Festival) in Cottbus, and Görlitz and Dessau's applications to become 'European Capital of Culture' represent key projects in the cities we investigated in terms of the start of regeneration efforts and a strengthening of urban identification. A lack of success in applying to host these events has proven to be a severe test for the strategies chosen, however, i.e., the competition among different municipalities to be 'cultural cities'. Large strategic projects in cities without visioning processes can thus only temporarily have an orientational function for actors or help establish a consensus. Long-term orientation requires the embedding of such projects in a visioning process.

3.3 Cooperation among Actors and Modes of Governance

Based on a model of strategic planning, strategic alliances between actors from political, administrative, economic, and public sectors form an institutional platform which allows visions and projects to be linked to one another. New forms of cooperation between public and private actors have been discussed since the 1990s under the heading of 'public private partnerships' and 'project-oriented planning'. Strategic planning has thus been addressed in the context of a political governance debate about a change 'from government to governance'.

In analyzing the empirical results, it has become clear that in the cities we investigated state support policies on the one hand and civic and economic initiatives on the other hand play a key role in the initialization of strategic planning approaches. Such initiatives rarely emanate from a city's political leadership. The initiative to generate strategic visions of urban development often comes from representatives of industrial associations, companies, universities, and clubs within the cities. As leaders of cities' public administrations and political sectors, mayors commonly play a major role in strategy development, however. They can initiate and promote visioning processes and key projects (e.g., Cottbus), but they can block them as well (e.g., Stralsund and Dessau). Our empirical results have made it clear that local political and administrative leaders (mayors and departmental heads) have little interest in the public negotiation of long-term visions of urban development, as they feel this may limit both their scope of action and political legitimacy. This distrust of initiatives put forward by civil society points to the fact that political leaders have little desire to change their strongly hierarchical understanding of politics and governance.

As a whole, strategic planning is not merely a task for planning, but rather a profoundly political process, which is based on specific conditions that can not be assumed in many shrinking cities.

For more information see:
Kühn, M. & Fischer, S. (2010). *Strategische Stadtplanung. Strategiebildung in schrumpfenden Städten aus planungs- und politikwissenschaftlicher Perspektive.* Detmold: Rohn Verlag.

Typologies of the Built Environment and the Example of Urban Vulnerability Assessment

Andreas Blum, Karin Gruhler

1. Theoretical Considerations

Research on the built environment deals with a complex and interdisciplinary subject and, especially concerning the objective of sustainable development, multidimensional and multivariate approaches are needed. Hence, as in other fields of environmental research, linear approaches will usually not be appropriate for structuring a complex reality (de Haan, 2001), in particular if options for action on the microscale level are searched for. Statistical data tends to be very general and at best allows for estimates to be made on a large or medium-scale level, such as for a city as a whole or on the level of a national economy. In addition, a lot of statistical data often can not be broken down to the microscale (e.g., building blocks) and extensive on-site inventories are prohibitive in terms of the resources needed to carry them out.

For example, it is not possible to develop refurbishment programs on the basis of average energy consumption figures for the urban building stock. More specific analyses and assessments will only be possible when the urban built environment is defined in categories like housing, office, and industrial buildings, and in a more detailed form such as housing construction periods and types, etc. We would then be able to identify hot spots of energy consumption or saving potentials.

With this in mind, the work with typologies provides a multidimensional approach to structure a set of given objects with respect to specific relevant research questions. Types can therefore be defined from a theoretical perspective on the basis of conceptual considerations and experience, or based on statistical analysis and classification. A combined approach is commonly adopted for complex objects and research designs, often leading to "constructed types" (Kluge, 1999, p. 70).

In spatial research, typology-approaches are used to describe, model, analyze, benchmark, and monitor the built environment with respect to buildings, infrastructure, and the urban structure. Typologies of the built environment offer a consistent set of (pre-)defined representative buildings, building blocks, and urban structures that have specific properties regarding issues like embodied resources, energy demands, typical land-coverage, and infrastructure demands, as well as the consumption of resources for renovation, and waste streams to be expected in case of demolition. Building typologies, for example, classify buildings in terms of construction periods and technologies. Urban structure types classify basic urban

B. Müller, *German Annual of Spatial Research and Policy 2010*,
German Annual of Spatial Research and Policy,
DOI 10.1007/978-3-642-12785-4_17, © Springer-Verlag Berlin Heidelberg 2011

spatial units that have a morphological and functionally homogenous character, which is defined by characteristic structures and development patterns of buildings, infrastructures, and open spaces.

Building typologies support large-scale inventories as well as microscale rapid assessments and may even provide quick information on easy-to-apply good practice solutions. A typology of urban structures can support highly aggregated models of the urban built environment for a national economy or an entire city, as well as for the microscale screening of stocks and flows on neighborhood levels or for housing market segments. When combined with scenario-techniques, it is also possible to illustrate the short and long-term effects of planning and development decisions.

As a methodology, typologies can generally be applied for empirical analysis in two ways. Firstly, they are a means of estimating a given empirical object (e.g., a building) with respect to specific characteristics by comparison with pre-defined types (of buildings). Secondly, typologies (e.g., of typical building blocks) can be used for the aggregate modeling and fast screening of characteristics of a superordinate system (e.g., an entire city) by representing relevant typical elements of this system with typical characteristics.

In an interdisciplinary context, typologies of the built environment can be utilized from three perspectives:

(a) Direct link: For research that focuses on the spatial and material physis of the urban built environment (e.g., land use, material input, energetic properties, etc.) and its evaluation and development, typologies of the built environment are directly linked with the object of investigation (e.g., Gruhler, Böhm, & Deilmann, 2006).

(b) Vehicle: For spatial research that does not directly deal with material or physical issues of the built environment. An example is given by socio-economic research on the housing preferences of citizens or on demographic change in different sectors of the housing market (e.g., Banse & Effenberger, 2008). Typologies of the built environment can serve as a vehicle to link socio-economic research and results with categories of urban planning.

(c) Interface: For interdisciplinary spatial research, a primarily morphologically defined typology of the built environment can serve as an intermediate starting point and synoptic focus for the definition of a shared subject (e.g., Siedentop, Schiller, Gutsche, Koziol, & Walther, 2006). Typologies from this perspective can be seen as a "boundary object" (Bowker & Star, 1999) that serves as an interface for communication, projection, and the integration of multi-criteria analysis.

In the following paragraph work with typologies for the built environment is presented with a 'direct link' example from recent research within the VERIS-Elbe Project (VERIS-Elbe: Changes and Management of Risks of Extreme Flood Events in Large River Basins – Illustrated by the River Elbe).[1]

---

1   For more information see Naumann et al. within this volume at pp. 89.

2. An Example

An example of the application of the typology approach in spatial research is the use of urban structure types that combine building types with typical urban development patterns for a finely graded spatial and temporal modeling of flood damage potentials in the built environment. The objective of the work package within the 'VERIS-Elbe Project' was the determination of regional specific depth-damage functions for flood-prone urban areas along the German Elbe River basin. A GIS-based flood damage model (Neubert, Naumann, & Deilmann, 2008) was developed for the residential building stock that allows for the simulation of different flood-scenarios and an estimation of the respective damage costs. For the simulation the residential building stock of the investigation area was differentiated into characteristic building types along typical construction technologies (timber frame, solid/bricks, etc.), periods of construction, and spatial patterns (single/two-family homes, apartment blocks, etc.) (see Fig. 1). As a result, specific damage types and repair costs for building construction and building services were integrated into the model as synthetic depth-damage functions. According to the simulated water levels and investigated building types it is now possible to determine specific flood damage and to calculate the respective costs of repair. Through the use of urban structure types, specific building type damage potentials can then be aggregated and simulated for larger settlement structures within investigation areas.

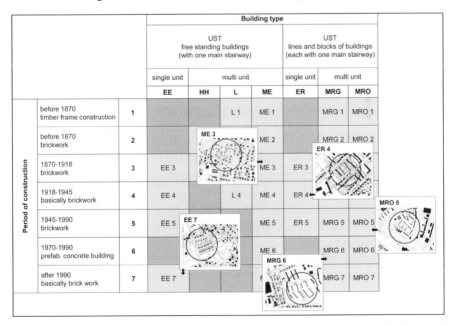

Fig. 1: Matrix and examples of urban structure types adapted from the VERIS-Elbe flood damage model. Source: Naumann, Nikolowski, and Golz (2009), p. 16.

References

Banse, J. & Effenberger, K.-H. (2008). Wohnungsnachfrage in den städtischen Teilmärkten der Stadt Dresden. In I. Iwanow (ed.), *Struktureller Wandel der Wohnungsnachfrage in schrumpfenden Städten und Regionen. Analyse und Prognose von Wohnpräferenzen, Neubaupotenzialen und Wohnungsleerständen* (pp. 63-98). Berlin: LIT.

Bowker, G. C. & Star, S. L. (1999). *Sorting Things Out: Classification and its Consequences*. Cambridge: MIT Press.

Gruhler, K., Böhm, R. & Deilmann, C. (2006). Stadtgebietsentwicklungen – Entwicklungsszenarien für Kommunen. *BundesBauBlatt, 55(2)*, pp. 11-13.

De Haan, G., Lantermann, E.-D., Linneweber, V. & Reusswig, F. (eds.) (2001). *Typenbildung in der sozialwissenschaftlichen Umweltforschung*. Opladen: Leske + Budrich.

Kluge, S. (1999). *Empirisch begründete Typenbildung. Zur Konstruktion von Typen und Typologien in der qualitativen Sozialforschung*. Opladen: Leske + Budrich.

Naumann, T., Nikolowski, J. & Golz, S. (2009). Synthetic Depth-damage Functions – A Detailed Tool for Analysing Flood Resilience of Building Types. In E. Pasche, N. Evelpidou, C. Zevenbergen, R. Ashley & S. Garvin (eds.), *Road Map Towards a Flood Resilient Urban Environment. Proceedings Final Conference of the COST action C 22 Urban Flood Management in Cooperation with UNESCO-IHP* (p. 16). Hamburg: University of Technology.

Neubert, M., Naumann, T. & Deilmann, C. (2008). Synthetic Water Level Building Damage Relationship for GIS-supported Flood Vulnerability Modeling of Residential Properties. In P. Samuels, S. Huntington, W. Allsop, & J. Harrop (eds.), *Flood Risk Management – Research and Practice. Proceedings of the European Conference on Flood Risk Management Research into Practice* (FLOODrisk 2008) (CD-ROM), Oxford/UK. Boca Raton: CRC Press.

Siedentop, S., Schiller, G., Gutsche, J. M., Koziol, M. & Walther, J. (2006). Siedlungsentwicklung und Infrastrukturfolgekosten. Bilanzierung und Strategieentwicklung. *BBR-Online-Publikationen, 3/2006*. Bonn: Bundesamt für Bauwesen und Raumordnung.

Appendix

List of Authors

Andreas Blum

Born in Nordhorn, Germany in 1960. He studied sociology, urban planning, and community development at the Technical University of Darmstadt. Since 1993 he has worked as a senior researcher at the Leibniz Institute of Ecological and Regional Development (IOER) in Dresden. He has also periodically worked as an assistant lecturer at the Dresden University of Technology since 1994. His research interests, among other things, include diverse aspects of evaluation, communication, and cooperation within projects involving sustainable development of the built environment.
a.blum@ioer.de

Joachim Burdack

Born in Berlin, Germany in 1951. He is head of the department for Regional Geography of Europe at the Leibniz Institute of Regional Geography (IfL) in Leipzig and Professor of Geography at the University of Leipzig. His current research interests include the development of metropolitan areas in Eastern and Western Europe, questions of regional development in Europe, and the problems small towns in rural areas have.
j_burdack@ifl-leipzig.de

Sonja Deppisch

Born in Schweinfurt, Germany in 1975. Since 2008 she has been the head of the social-ecological research group *Climate Change and Spatial Development – plan B:altic* at HafenCity University Hamburg (HCU). She was a lecturer on European spatial development at Leibniz University Hanover as well as on climate change and regional development at HCU. Before joining HCU she worked for the Leibniz Institute of Ecological and Regional Development (IOER) in Dresden and the European Commission. She obtained a PhD in planning from the Faculty for Architecture and Landscape Sciences at the Leibniz University Hanover in 2007. Her main research fields are resilience to climate change and spatial planning, planning theory and ethical questions, transdisciplinary research, as well as cross-border governance. She is a member of the ARL-Youth Forum.
sonja.deppisch@hcu-hamburg.de

B. Müller, *German Annual of Spatial Research and Policy 2010*,
German Annual of Spatial Research and Policy,
DOI 10.1007/978-3-642-12785-4, © Springer-Verlag Berlin Heidelberg 2011

Fabian Dosch

Degree in geography studies with geophysical orientation, PhD in natural sciences. He is currently a senior project manager at Division I 5 Transport and the Environment at the German Federal Institute for Research on Building, Urban Affairs and Spatial Development (BBSR). He is mainly involved with the development of sustainable land use strategies, regional and local adaptation policies on climate change, project management, and policy advice.
fabian.dosch@bbr.bund.de

Sebastian Ebert

Born in Berlin, Germany in 1977. He is a research fellow at the Academy for Spatial Research and Planning (ARL) in Hanover and Research Coordinator of the EU-project *BalticClimate*. His current focus is on the mitigation of and adaptation to climate change in rural areas as well as on small and medium-sized towns, especially in the Baltic Sea region. Within this field, a special topic is local and regional development strategies generated by climate change. Further research activities include the improvement of transnational communication abilities on planning systems and planning terms.
ebert@arl-net.de

Susen Fischer

Born in Eisenach, Germany in 1979. She is a scientific researcher at the Leibniz Institute for Regional Development and Structural Planning (IRS) in Erkner. Her current research interests include the analysis of local and regional politics, strategies for urban regeneration, as well as the integration of immigrants in urban and rural communities.
fischers@irs-net.de

Enke Franck

Born in Kiel, Germany in 1974. She studied economic geography, spatial planning, and law and administrative science at the University of Mainz and University of Hanover. She worked for seven years in regional and state planning in Lower Saxony before becoming a research assistant at the Academy for Spatial Research and Planning (ARL) in Hanover in January 2009, where she took over coordination of the research program IMPLAN (Climate change and spatial planning in Lower

Saxony), part of the Lower Saxony Ministry for Science and Culture's cooperation KLIFF (Climate impact and adaptation research in Lower Saxony). The focus of her current work is on climate adaptation measures in regional planning in Lower Saxony.
franck@arl-net.de

Manfred Fuhrich

Born in Hamburg, Germany in 1950. He studied architecture, sociology, and urban and regional planning in Berlin. He has a PhD in urban planning from the TU Berlin. He is head of the Urban Development unit at the Federal Institute for Research on Building, Urban Affairs and Spatial Development (BBSR) in the Federal Office for Building and Regional Planning (BBR) in Bonn. He worked as a trainee in a large housing association and was a fellow at the Technical University of Hamburg. He has been active in the field of experimental housing and urban planning for more than two decades with a focus on housing estates, ecologic building, urban renewal, indicators in urban affairs, sustainable development, and qualities of living in urban quarters.
manfred.fuhrich@bbr.bund.de

Ludger Gailing

Born in Dortmund, Germany in 1976. He studied spatial planning at the Universities of Dortmund and Grenoble. Since 2003 he has been a scientific researcher and project coordinator at the Leibniz Institute for Regional Development and Structural Planning (IRS) in Erkner. His research interests include regional governance, the social construction of cultural landscapes, as well as institutional change in regional development. His work concentrates on the application of theoretical principles underlying institutions, governance, and paths when analyzing cultural landscapes as common goods, and the examination of case studies of regional policy and institutional arrangements in river landscapes, suburban areas, and rural landscapes.
gailing@irs-net.de

Evi Goderbauer

Born in Munich, Germany in 1967. She studied urban and regional planning in Berlin. She works in the Urban Development department at the Federal Institute for Research on Building, Urban Affairs and Spatial Development (BBSR) in the Federal Office for Building and Regional Planning (BBR) in Bonn. She previously

worked as a town planner in local government. She is currently involved in research on housing and urban redevelopment with a focus on urban restructuring in western Germany.
evi.goderbauer@bbr.bund.de

Sebastian Golz

Born in Forst, Germany in 1980. He studied civil engineering at the Technical University of Dresden. He has been a research associate at the Leibniz Institute of Ecological and Regional Development (IOER) in Dresden since 2008, and is involved in the research *Environmental Risks in Urban and Regional Development* and the *Resource Efficiency of Settlement Structures*. His current research interests include damage to buildings caused by flooding, as well as the validation of precautionary and adaptation measures to building structures as a result of climate change.
s.golz@ioer.de

Karin Gruhler

Born in Hoym, Germany in 1961. She studied architecture and urban planning at the Technische Universität Dresden. Since 1992 she has worked as a senior researcher at the Leibniz Institute of Ecological and Regional Development (IOER) in Dresden. Her main fields of work are the analysis of urban structures on the basis of building types, urban structure types, and material and energy balances, and life cycle assessments for the built environment.
k.gruhler@ioer.de

Gérard Hutter

Born in Wuppertal, Germany in 1966. He studied economics at the University of Duisburg, he has a PhD in Geography, and has worked on strategy development for cities and regions since 1996. He has worked on projects within the scope of the *Joint Initiative for Research and Innovation*, supported by German federal and state governments, and European research projects (e.g., Integrated Project as part of the European Commission's *Sixth Framework Programme*). He is involved in the *AESOP Thematic Group about Resilience and Risk Mitigation Strategies* and is also a guest editor for a special issue concerning resilience and planning.
g.hutter@ioer.de

Heiderose Kilper

Born in Stuttgart, Germany in 1953. Director of the Leibniz Institute for Regional Development and Structural Planning (IRS) in Erkner. She has the chair for Urban and Regional Development in the Faculty of Architecture, Civil Engineering, and Urban Planning at the Technical University of Cottbus. From 2002 to 2005 she was director of an extra-university research institute at the University of Hanover and had a chair in the Department of Landscape Planning and Nature Conservation. Her fields of research include governance/European multi-level systems, theories of planning and regulating, structural and developmental policies for regions, cultural landscapes, and federalism in the German Federal Republic.
kilper@irs-net.de

Manfred Kühn

Born in Gießen, Germany in 1960. He is a scientific researcher at the Leibniz Institute for Regional Development and Structural Planning (IRS) in Erkner and teaches at the Institute for Geography at the University of Potsdam. He holds a PhD in economic and social science. His current research interests include the analysis of urban and regional planning, and strategies for urban regeneration and regional development.
kuehnm@irs-net.de

Thilo Lang

Has studied and worked in Stuttgart, Kaiserslautern, Hamburg, Berlin, Sheffield and Durham (UK) before becoming deputy head of the department for Regional Geography of Europe at the Leibniz Institute for Regional Geography (IfL) in Leipzig in 2009. He holds a PhD in human geography. His current research interests include post-disciplinary comparative urban studies, socio-spatial processes of multiple peripheralization, innovation and socio-economic development in areas outside of metropolitan regions, as well as urban decline and urban regeneration. He is co-editor of the German online-journal *Städte im Umbruch*.
t_lang@ifl-leipzig.de

Bastian Lange

Born in Ruit-Ostfildern, Germany in 1970. He holds a PhD in Geography. Since 2006 he has been a postdoctoral researcher and project manager at the Leibniz Institute for Regional Geography (IfL) in Leipzig. Current projects include the EU project *ACRE* as well as the *First Creative Industries Report* for the State of Saxony. Further research fields are the creative and knowledge industries, knowledge milieu studies, entrepreneurship, and theories of space and governance. Since 2001 he has taught at universities in Berlin, Potsdam, Kassel, und Leipzig. His most recent publications include *Die Räume der Kreativszenen: Culturepreneurs und ihre Orte in Berlin*, and *Governance der Kreativwirtschaft*, written together with Ares Kalandides, Dr. Birgit Stöber, and Inga Wellmann.
Bastian.Lange@berlin.de

Bernhard Müller

Director of the Dresden-based Leibniz Institute of Ecological and Regional Development (IOER), Professor of Spatial Development at the Technische Universität Dresden and Vice President of the Leibniz Association. He is a member of the German Academy of Science and Engineering (acatech), the Saxonian Academy of Sciences, and the German Academy for Spatial Research and Planning (ARL). Professor Müller is also initiator and head of the Managing Board of the internationally-oriented Dresden Leibniz Graduate School (DLGS), which deals with issues of resilience in urban and regional development, especially regarding demographic, climate, and economic change. He is also the project leader of the Dresden based *REGKLAM* project on climate change adaption.
b.mueller@ioer.de

Thomas Naumann

Born in Freital, Germany in 1971. After a professional education in the building industry he studied civil engineering at the Technical University of Dresden (TUD) until 1996. After three years in private practice he went into research and began working at the TUD's Institute of Building Construction, as a research associate. In 2006 he finished his PhD. Since 2005 he has been a research associate at the Leibniz Institute of Ecological and Regional Development (IOER) in Dresden, doing research in the research area *Environmental Risks in Urban and Regional Development*. He is also a partner at an engineering firm that specializes in damage analysis and expertise. Since 2005 he has also acted as an assistant lecturer at the TUD, lecturing on types of building damage and techniques of refurbishment.
t.naumann@ioer.de

Johannes Nikolowski

Born in Groß-Gerau, Germany in 1980. He studied civil engineering at the Technical University of Dresden. Since 2007 he has been a member of the research staff at the Leibniz Institute of Ecological and Regional Development (IOER) in Dresden in the research area *Environmental Risks in Urban and Regional Development*. His current research interests include damage to buildings due to flooding as well as the validation of precautionary and adaptation measures to building structures as a consequence of climate change.
j.nikolowski@ioer.de

Alfred Olfert

Born in Almaty, Republic of Kazakhstan in 1974. He studied geography, soil ecology, forest ecology, and landscape planning at the Dresden University of Technology and Charles University in Prague. He has worked as a research associate at the Leibniz Institute of Ecological and Regional Development (IOER) in Dresden since 2003. His scientific work is concentrated on the field of risk and multi-risk research, with an emphasis on flooding, risk reduction, and evaluation. He is currently in charge of scientific management for the *REGKLAM* joint research project.
a.olfert@ioer.de

Jana Planek

Born in Dresden, Germany in 1980. She has studied geography, biology and forest ecology at the Dresden University of Technology. She has worked as research associate at the Leibniz Institute of Ecological and Regional Development (IOER) in Dresden since 2008. She was a staff member at the *REGKLAM* Regional Office for Coordination.
j.planek@ioer.de

Lars Porsche

Born in Dortmund, Germany in 1972. He studied geography at the Ruhr-Universität Bochum and the University of Zaragoza. He subsequently worked for Soluziona, Unión FENOSA in the area of strategic urban planning in Spain and the Philippines. He then worked freelance for the GPE Gesellschaft für Projektmanagement und Grundstücksentwicklung mbH on a project which was part of the *5th EU Research Framework Programme*. Since 2002 he has been a project manager at the Federal Institute for Research on Building, Urban Affairs and Spatial Development (BBSR).

The focus of his work and research is on energy and spatial development, renewable energy, integrated local and regional energy concepts, cultural landscape development, and urban climate protection and adaptation.
lars.porsche@bbr.bund.de

Andreas Röhring

Born in Klosterheide, Germany in 1958. He studied at the Friedrich List University of Transport and Communications in Dresden. From 1987 to 1990 he was a scientific assistant at the Research Center for Territorial Planning in Berlin. He joined the Leibniz Institute for Regional Development and Structural Planning (IRS) in Erkner in 1992. His research focuses on the conversion of former military sites, correlations between water protection and land use, and the development of cultural landscapes as action arenas from a theoretical and application-oriented perspective.
roehring@irs-net.de

Mareike Schaerffer

Born in Hamburg, Germany in 1979. She has been a researcher at HafenCity University Hamburg (HCU) since 2007, contributing to international projects on risk perception in flood-prone areas and climate adaptation governance. She was awarded a diploma in environmental sciences from the University of Lüneburg in 2006. From 2006 until 2007 she worked as a researcher at the Technical University of Hamburg-Harburg, dealing with the implementation of the *EU Water Framework Directive* while focusing on European port cities. Her main research fields are planning processes in river catchment areas, resilient cities, and climate adaptation governance. The theme of her PhD thesis is citizen engagement in planning processes that are concerned with flood protection. She is a member of the ARL-Youth Forum.
mareike.schaerffer@hcu-hamburg.de

Reinhard Schinke

Born in Dresden, Germany in 1970. He studied civil engineering at the Technical University of Dresden and obtained his doctoral degree from the Brandenburg University of Technology in Cottbus. He has been a member of the research staff at the Leibniz Institute of Ecological and Regional Development (IOER) in Dresden since 2007, and is active in the research area Environmental Risks in Urban and Regional Development. His main research interests include the analysis of damage

to buildings caused by floods and rising groundwater, as well as the assessment of precautionary measures for building structures as a consequence of these natural hazards.
r.schinke@ioer.de

Stephan Schmidt

Born in Berlin, Germany in 1981. He is a human geographer with a special interest in spatial development, peripheral regions, and sustainability in the context of Northern and Central Europe. He studied at the University of Greifswald, Germany, and is now working on his dissertation in Basel, Switzerland. His current position is affiliated with the Program Sustainability Research at the University of Basel and focuses on the *Neue Regionalpolitik* of Switzerland and its impacts on sustainable regional development.
stephan.schmidt@unibas.ch

Frank Sondershaus

Born in Nuremberg, Germany in 1979. He studied geography (major), political science, and sociology at Erlangen University, graduating in 2007. His thesis (Magister) explored the obstacles to sustainable regional development in administratively divided areas. After completing his studies, he began working on the project *Linking precautionary flood protection to the development of regional cultural landscapes in river landscapes: An analysis taking into account the effects of climate change on low water levels* at the Institute for Regional Development and Structural Planning (IRS) in Erkner. His particular focus in this project has been on issues of declining water levels. At present he is investigating climate-adaptive water management in small river basins.
sondershaus@irs-net.de

Torsten Thurmann

Born in Wuppertal, Germany in 1978. He studied landscape planning at the University of Hanover from 1999 to 2005. During a one-year period of study at the University of the West of England in Bristol he also studied urban and regional planning. From 2005 to 2008 he worked at the East Midlands Regional Development Agency in Nottingham, England as a consultant on a variety of urban and regional development issues. Since 2009 he has worked as a personal assistant to Professor Heiderose Kilper at the Leibniz Institute for Regional Development and Structural

Planning (IRS) in Erkner. Since 2008 he has also worked as a research assistant at the chair for Urban and Regional Development at the Brandenburg Technical University (BTU) Cottbus. He is currently working on a PhD project dealing with learning processes and conflicts in the International Building Exhibition *IBA Fürst-Pückler-Land*.
thurmann@irs-net.de

Andreas Vetter

Born in Altdöbern, Germany in 1975. He studied at the Technical University Berlin, where he graduated in landscape planning. In 2006 he finished a two-year traineeship and took the State Exam in landscape planning at the District Government of Cologne. He then began work as a research assistant at the Leibniz Institute for Regional Development and Structural Planning (IRS) in Erkner, where he was involved in different research projects regarding the regional development of cultural landscapes, with an emphasis on institutional frameworks. His projects there focused on the specific challenges of river landscapes and post-mining landscapes. He now works at the German Federal Environment Agency (Umweltbundesamt, UBA) in the field of adaptation to climate change.
andreas.vetter@uba.de

Portrait of the Editors' Institutions

Academy for Spatial Research and Planning (ARL)

The ARL is concerned with research on spatial structures and developments that are important for Germany and of international relevance. The ARL is a service institution for basic and application-oriented research. At the same time, it is a neutral forum which promotes discourse about spatial science issues. The ARL network currently consists of approximately 1,000 experts. Their tasks are, among other things, to initiate research and to perform joint research within this network, as well as to encourage a knowledge transfer between spatial research and planning practice.

Academy for Spatial Research and Planning (ARL)
Leibniz Forum for Spatial Sciences
Hohenzollernstr. 11
30161 Hannover

E-Mail: ARL@ARL-net.de
Internet: www.ARL-net.de
President 2009/2010: Prof. Dr. Hans H. Blotevogel
Secretary General: Prof. Dr. Dietmar Scholich

Federal Institute for Research on Building, Urban Affairs and Spatial Development (BBSR)

The Federal Institute for Research on Building, Urban Affairs and Spatial Development (BBSR) within the Federal Office for Building and Regional Planning (BBR) is a departmental research institution in the portfolio of the German Federal Ministry of Transport, Building and Urban Affairs (BMVBS). It supports the federal government with sectoral scientific consultation in the political areas of spatial planning, urban development, housing, and building at the national and European level.

Federal Institute for Research on Building, Urban Affairs and Spatial Development
(BBSR) within the Federal Office for Building and Regional Planning (BBR)
Deichmanns Aue 31-37
53179 Bonn

E-Mail: bbsr@bbr.bund.de
Internet: www.bbsr.bund.de
Director: Prof. Elke Pahl-Weber

Leibniz Institute for Regional Geography (IfL)

The Leibniz Institute for Regional Geography (IfL) pursues basic research into regional geography of Europe and provides – as one part of its educational task – geographic information about spatial structures and their development. The international studies of the IfL concentrate on Central and Eastern Europe, but also include a Europe-wide comparative perspective. By rethinking and further developing theories and concepts of traditional Regional Geography, the IfL contributes to an enhanced understanding of spatial organisation and spatial practices of European societies.

Leibniz Institute for Regional Geography (IfL)
Schongauerstr. 9
04329 Leipzig

E-Mail: info@ifl-leipzig.de
Internet: www.ifl-leipzig.de
Director: Prof. Dr. Sebastian Lentz

Leibniz Institute of Ecological and Regional Development (IOER)

The Leibniz Institute of Ecological and Regional Development (IOER) carries out interdisciplinary research into the complex interaction of the natural, built, and social environments. Core areas of research are Landscape Change and Management, Resource Efficiency of Settlement Structures, Environmental Risks in Urban and Regional Development, as well as the Monitoring of Settlement and Open Space Development.

Leibniz Institute of Ecological and Regional Development (IOER)
Weberplatz 1
01217 Dresden

E-Mail: info@ioer.de
Internet: www.ioer.de
Director: Prof. Dr. Dr. h.c. Bernhard Müller

Leibniz Institute for Regional Development and Structural Planning (IRS)

The Leibniz Institute for Regional Development and Structural Planning (IRS) in Erkner researches social, economic, and spatial aspects of urban and regional development and its governance. It investigates the transformation and governance of cities and regions from a social science perspective. With its research projects the institute contributes actively to devising objectives and strategies for the development and stabilisation of European subregions.

Leibniz Institute for Regional Development and Structural Planning (IRS)
Flakenstr. 28-31
15537 Erkner

E-Mail: regional@irs-net.de
Internet: www.irs-net.de
Director: Prof. Dr. Heiderose Kilper

Printing: Ten Brink, Meppel, The Netherlands
Binding: Stürtz, Würzburg, Germany